GOGOL

From a painting by Moller

GOGOL

GOGOL

By

Janko Lavrin

Author of *Dostoevsky and his Creation, Ibsen and his Creation, Nietzsche and Modern Consciousness, Tolstoy, etc.*

HASKELL HOUSE PUBLISHERS LTD.
Publishers of Scarce Scholarly Books
NEW YORK. N. Y. 10012
1973

HASKELL HOUSE PUBLISHERS LTD.
Publishers of Scarce Scholarly Books
280 LAFAYETTE STREET
NEW YORK, N. Y. 10012

Library of Congress Cataloging in Publication Data

Lavrin, Janko, 1887-
Gogol.

Reprint of the 1926 ed., issued in series: The Republic of letters.
"Chronological list of Gogol's works": p.
Bibliography: p.
1. Gogol', Nikolaĭ Vasil'evich, 1809-1852.
I. Series: The Republic of letters.
PG3335.L28 1973 891.7'8'309 72-2123
ISBN 0-8383-1473-2

Printed in the United States of America

CONTENTS

NOTE

The object of the present book is to introduce to English readers a great and complex foreign writer in as simple terms as possible. As this it the first extensive study of Gogol in English, I had to consider chiefly the general characteristics of the man and his work, avoiding those issues which are of more special interest.

Quotations referred to in this book are taken from the following English versions :

The Overcoat and Other Stories, and *The Dead Souls*, translated by Mrs. Constance Garnett (*Chatto & Windus*) ; *Taras Bulba and Other Stories* (Everyman's Library) ; *Stories from Russian Authors*, translated by R. S. Townsend (Everyman's Library) ; *The Inspector-General*, translated by A. Sykes (W. Scott). Extracts from the letters, as well as from several stories, have been translated by myself.

November, 1925. J.L.

GOGOL

Chapter One

GOGOL AND RUSSIAN LITERATURE

I

The hero of an old Russian saga, Ilya of Murom, was lame until he was thirty. But by a miracle he suddenly recovered and showed so much strength that he soon defeated the mightiest *bogatyrs* (heroes) and, in spite of his humble origin, attained to the highest honours at the court of Prince Vladimir.

This saga is in a way symbolic of Russian literature. Owing chiefly to Tartar invasion and its consequences, the literary genius of Russia remained for centuries inactive and as it were paralyzed. There flourished an astoundingly rich folk-lore among the peasants, yet the development of a literature in the European sense was stopped, in spite of its splendid beginnings in the twelfth century which produced such works as the Chronicle of the monk Nestor* and the *Song of Igor's Raid*.** From the Tartar invasion to the end of the seventeenth century Russia was practically severed from the rest of Europe. Having no direct contact either with its politics or its culture, she seemed to be lying under a thick crust of eternal snow which would not melt and give way to a new spring. And the Russian literature of those ages of suffering, chaos and stagnation is almost as barren as the Russian steppes. Its most notable production was written in the second half of the seventeenth century and bears the title, *The Life of the Archpriest Avvakum Written by Himself*. Apart from being a unique document of its times, this autobiography reveals by its style and verve a powerful though narrow-minded personality.*** While France, Italy and England could already boast of a great literary past, the literature of Russia was negligible. Moreover, the very language used by it was a rather artificial mixture of the spoken Russian and of that dead old-Slavonic tongue which plays the same part in the Russian Church as Latin does among the Roman Catholics.

* He was born in 1056 and died c. 1117.

** *Slovo o polku Igorevie*, c. 1186.

*** The Archpriest Avvakum, a fanatic " old-believer " and opponent of Patriarch Nikon's innovations, was burnt " for his great offence of the Tsar's house " in 1681.

It was the epoch of reforms initiated by Peter the Great that made conscious efforts to adopt the living speech alone as the proper medium for literature. The first important figure and the father of modern literature is Lomonossov (1712-1765), a remarkable and many-sided personality, active as a poet, savant and publicist. Though far from being a poetical genius, he had an instinctive feeling for all the beauties and the potential strength of his native tongue which he commanded with greater ability and more understanding than any of his contemporaries or immediate followers.

"Charles V," he wrote "used to say that with God one ought to converse in Spanish, with a friend in French, with enemies in German, and with women in Italian. Had he known Russian he certainly would have added that in this language one could suitably talk to all of them. For he would find in it the majesty of Spanish, the liveliness of French, the strength of German, the tenderness of Italian, and together with all this the wealth, as well as the exact precision, of Latin and Greek."

Those who know Russian will hardly deny that Lomonossov's judgment was right. Yet it took more than a hundred years of toil before this powerful language was entirely freed from the bondage of its dead old-Slavonic parent, and produced a literature worthy of it. In the third decade of the nineteenth century the Russian literary tongue could already compete with most of her grown-up European sisters, and only a few years later the French author, Prosper Mérimée, who was more or less acquainted with Russian and translated from Pushkin and Gogol, wrote: "It is the richest of all European languages. It is endowed with a marvellous gift for clearness and concision. One single word is enough to connect several ideas which in another tongue would require whole phrases. It is only the French language, based as it is on Greek and Latin and strengthened by all its northern and southern dialects—in short, the language of Rabelais—that can give us a notion of its subtlety and force."

II

The period from Peter the Great to the end of Catherine II, that is, the whole of the eighteenth century, was chiefly a period of literary experiments, clumsy imitations, adaptations, and of all mortal sins that can be committed upon a living tongue. The wigged and powdered versifiers, graduates of the French pseudo-Classic school, swore by Boileau and wrote according to his rules—by the sweat of their brows. The Russian language often looked in their industrious hands like a sturdy, red-cheeked peasant girl who had been rouged, arrayed in second-hand stage robes, and ordered to move with pompous dignity. The young literary market of Russia was flooded with hollow-sounding odes, epics (various " Petriades " and " Rossiades "), and copies of French tragedies, most of which are now entirely forgotten. Some poems by the really gifted Derzhavin (1743-1816) and Denis Fon-Vizin's (1744-92) two comedies, *The Brigadier* and *Th: Minor*—this is all that has remained and probably will remain from that epoch which was heroic by its toil rather than by its creation.

This preparatory period was soon enlarged by new Western influences and fashions. Thus towards the end of the eighteenth century, Karamzin (1766-1826), the first significant prose-writer, introduced—through his *Poor Lizzie* (1792) and his *Letters of a Travelling Russian* (1791-92)—the so-called sentimental trend, under the strong influence of Rousseau and partly also that of Sterne. Yet this faithful pupil of Rousseau wrote, later on, a voluminous *History of the Russian Empire* in an entirely conservative vein : a kind of glorification of autocracy. He is important at present only in so far as he represents the transition between the artificial period of Catherine II and that of Alexander I which soon produced great and unexpected poetic achievements. It was the prose-writer Karamzin who gave the final sanction to the living Russian speech freed from church-Slavonic archaisms, and in this effort he was followed by the younger generation, the most notable representatives of which are Krylov (1768-1844) and Zhukovsky (1783-1852).

Krylov is the Russian La Fontaine. Although he has not the polished elegance of his French master, he filled the pseudo-Classic form of the fable with Russian style and spirit. He is impressive by his straightforward naturalness, his subdued humour and satire, and particularly by the laconic virility of his language, which he took direct from the treasury of the folk-speech, preserving all its flavour, all its plastic power. Together with Griboyedov (1795-1829), the author of the great comedy— *Gore ot Uma* (*The Misfortune of Being Clever*), Krylov is the most epigrammatic Russian poet. Zhukovsky, on the other hand, summed up all the technical and musical attainments of his predecessors with the skill of a supreme virtuoso. In his hands the Russian literary language became a symphonic orchestra. As its first able conductor, Zhukovsky showed its strength not so much in original works, as in his excellent translations from English and German poets, and later of Homer's

Odyssey. His adaptability was so surprising that some of his translations read even better than the originals. And so Maurice Baring is hardly wrong in calling him " the first and the best translator in European literature."

Zhukovsky did all he could to undermine the lingering remainders of pseudo-Classic taste and tradition. Anxious to widen the range of Russian poetry proper, he tried to find new sources of inspiration in the poetry of Germany and England. Sentimental and romantic, steeped in Western poetry as well as in the Russian folklore, he is one of the most important pioneers and representatives of that period which culminated in the genius of Alexander Pushkin.

III

The advent of Pushkin (1799-1837) coincided with the great uplift of Russia which took place after the French invasion of 1812. The war with Napoleon stirred up the whole country to its very marrow, whilst the final victory over him aroused national self-consciousness and all kinds of latent energies. The subsequent stay of the Russian army in Paris revealed, moreover, to many young officers those liberal principles which had formed the theoretic background of the French

Revolution. This dangerous contraband of ideas was smuggled into Russia where it continued to spread after the conclusion of the so-called Holy Alliance.

The Emperor Alexander I was not great enough to perceive the real needs of his time. He began as a well-meaning liberal monarch and finished as an eastern despot. Yet all his reactionary measures could not weed out the new spirit which found its shelter in various secret societies and led to the abortive rising of December 14th, 1825. After a complete rout of those dreamers who claimed for Russia a constitution, abolition of serfdom, and some of them even a republic, the iron rule of Nicholas I plunged the country into a long political stagnation. The very word "freedom" was banished from the Russian vocabulary. The watchful bureaucracy raised once more a Chinese wall between Russia and Europe, a wall whose function was to bar out the slightest breeze of political fresh air from abroad. The years between 1825 and 1855 were those of a stifling nightmare, of corruption, of banishments, of persecutions, and executions. The young poet Ryleyev was executed, Dostoevsky was sent to Siberia for penal servitude, the Ukrainian poet Shevchenko was doomed to pine away as a simple soldier on the Asiatic frontier, while such a talented publicist as

Alexander Hertzen was compelled to seek refuge abroad. Pushkin himself had to suffer both from the régime and the general atmosphere; so had Lermontov, and the critic Bielinsky.

Fortunately, the spirit once awakened could not be exorcised even by the strictest orders and measures from above. Banished from the public life of Russia, it showed all the greater vitality in literature. It was under the reign of Nicholas I, that the Golden Age of Russian poetry (1820–1830) bore its finest fruits, and that the first great harvest of Russian prose took place. Literature was in fact the only domain left to the cultured Russian as a means of self-expression, and so he could not help taking it up seriously—not only as a pleasure, but also as a disguised weapon against the "dark forces" which were stifling his own country. Pushkin matured and wrote his best works after 1825. And apart from Pushkin and his circle we can point out—to mention only the best names—such a remarkable individuality as Lermontov (1814-41), the Russian Burns—Koltsov (1808-42), and the first great prose-writer, Nikolai Gogol (1809-52). Turgenev, Dostoevsky, Goncharov, Tolstoy—they all started their literary career under Nicholas I. However, these representatives of the "Golden Age" of Russian prose, which reached its highest pitch under the liberal rule of

Alexander II, were already descendants and not actual founders : they developed, enlarged, modified and brought to perfection those elements which had been bequeathed to them first of all by Pushkin, by Lermontov's *Hero of our Times* (the first introspective novel in Russia), and by the works of Gogol.

Lermontov, the most romantic and self-centred of all Russian poets, died before he had time to mature and give all that one could expect from his rich and extravagant genius. And so the stress must be laid on Pushkin and Gogol as the two main pillars at the entrance to modern Russian literature. These two pillars are widely different in their material, their texture and colouring, yet they curiously complete each other. With all their differences, both of them are so great and at the same time so essentially " Russian " that for this very reason they are entitled to claim world-wide reputation.

IV

Both Pushkin and Gogol had numerous predecessors of minor importance. In addition to the names already mentioned, there were many other more or less talented poets whose fame was eclipsed by the appearance of Pushkin. Neither was prose neglected. Between Karamzin's *Poor Lizzie* and Gogol's literary achievements one can find a number of sentimental stories, didactic adventurous novels, and historical romances in the manner of Walter Scott. Naryezhny's *Russian Gil Blas* appeared in 1814. Bulgarin and Senkovsky–the two ex-Poles and notorious literary *canailles* of those days—became extremely prolific "best sellers". Then there was the exuberant Bestuzhev—Marlinsky who had the courage not only to write romances but also to live them. Zagoskin, too, sprang into sudden fame by his historical novel, *Jury Miloslavsky* (1829); while Pogodin, Polevoy, Count Sollogub and others made several attempts at depicting life in its more realistic aspects. However, all this has little value nowadays when measured by that standard which we apply to the work of Pushkin or Gogol.

The young Pushkin had been influenced for a time by Byron's works, but he soon turned from individual heroes as such to their actual background: to the *byt*,* the spirit and the traditions of real Russia. His great novel in verse, *Eugen Onyegin* (finished in 1831), is rather typical of this transition. At the same time, such pieces as

* An untranslatable Russian word which corresponds to the French *mœurs*, yet is broader.

GOGOL

The Negro of Peter the Great and particularly *The Captain's Daughter* are the first examples of prose-works every bit of which is Russian in the best sense of this word ; works in which classicism and realism meet, blending the truth of life with the truth of art in a harmonious and synthetic whole. Pushkin is always simple, always lucid, and full of that naturalness which excludes *a priori* anything that sounds false, didactic, stilted, or pompous.

If we now turn to Gogol, we find in him an artist utterly unlike Pushkin—that bright, affirmative genius of Russian literature. Contrary to him, Gogol sees above all the negative side of life. While Pushkin creates through expansion in the world he loves, Gogol can create only through reaction against that reality which makes him hate and suffer. Pushkin is the eternal youth, brimming with vitality, laughter and life. There is affirmation of life in his very sadness. In Gogol, however, we feel something enigmatic and disturbing even when he laughs—particularly when he laughs. His genius differs from that of Pushkin in the same way in which the beauty of the moon differs from the beauty of the sun. Pushkin is always divinely obvious, Gogol nearly always mysterious—even under the veil of extreme obviousness. Being organically simple, Pushkin transmutes reality by simplifying it : by toning down all its loud and exaggerated features. Gogol again lights up everything by a kind of nocturnal magic which grotesquely increases and distorts certain qualities at the expense of others. Pushkin creates his characters straightway—out of one piece as it were. Gogol, however, " makes " them first, almost as one makes puppets : he seems to construct them out of many pieces, and once they are ready in his vision, he fills them with life and with such intense reality of their own that they often pursue the reader like hallucinations.

Pushkin's strength is in his sense of proportion, that of Gogol very often in the absence of all measure and proportion. However much Pushkin might have been carried away by his themes, esthetically he was always detached enough to create with that higher objectivity which is the result of complete artistic freedom. The intensity of Gogol, however, is due above all to the fact that he is never a free and detached artist, but always struggling—struggling with himself, with life, and finally with his own art. He is the most egocentric of all Russian prose-writers. His vision of reality itself is entirely subjective, that is, regulated by his own inner needs and tendencies. And so is his language with all its immense variety of rhythm, of musical cadences, of ornament and colour. He revels in endless periods, in glowing descriptions, in metaphors and superlatives to such an extent as to be in danger of losing himself. Especially in his early stories he is always in the superlatives, and not seldom on the borderline between prose and poetry ; sometimes he even approaches the rhetorical oleograph. Yet his innate genius always saves him from esthetic pitfalls. The ebb and flow of his prose remind one of the sea-waves which can engulf sand, stones, and even mud, without losing a bit of their primeval majesty and beauty. Having an astounding sense for the musical value of words as such, Gogol struck upon many a new orchestral possibility of the Russian language.

To put it briefly, Pushkin's genius is Apollonian, and that of Gogol is Dionysian. Pushkin's art is always objective, while the art of Gogol is profoundly personal even in its apparent objectivity. Contrary to Pushkin's wholeness, Gogol is the first of those self-divided Russian writers in whom " all contradictions exist side by side ". His creative urge itself may have been due to his need of coping with such contradictions. He is also the first *seeker* (on a big and tragic scale) in Russian literature. In this respect Gogol is the psychological prototype of both Dostoevsky and Tolstoy, while Turgenev and Goncharov, for example, are more akin to the objective Pushkin, at least in so far as they never mix their art with any ethical struggle, with metaphysics or religion.

The divergence that existed between Gogol and Pushkin is in a way characteristic of the whole of Russian literature, including the modernists proper, as well as the " decadents ".

V

Gogol was, in essence, a diseased and too introspective genius. As such, he was always glad to lean on someone in order to be stimulated and feel confident of himself. And who could attract and fascinate him more than his opposite : the virile and all-sided Pushkin, who was brimming over with higher sanity ? Gogol felt in fact curiously drawn towards him, collaborated for a while in his *Sovremennik* (*The Contemporary*), listened to his useful advice in matters of art, and even received from him the themes for his own masterpieces, *The Revizor* and *The Dead Souls.* Pushkin again appreciated Gogol's talent from the very beginning. He encouraged him, revealed to him the value of the great foreign writers, especially that of Cervantes and Molière, probably influenced his taste, and helped him along in some practical matters as well. But it is significant that the expansive Pushkin could never be on quite friendly terms with the " sly Ukrainian ", as he called Gogol, who always puzzled his acquaintances with an excess of reserve and an innate tendency towards mystifications. However, the personal influence of Pushkin on Gogol must not be exaggerated, for in art the " sly Ukrainian " was too exclusive and too conceited to stand anybody's influence in the long run. The fact that he himself exaggerated it * proves not that he was right, but simply that he was fond of projecting into Pushkin those elements which he needed most as his own complement.

Gogol was in fact too full of various repressions, masks and contradictions to attract the immediate and lasting sympathies of a man such as Pushkin. Yet it was largely this chaotic and " dark " side of his character that was responsible for many aspects of his originality ; for it made him not only probe into painful inner conflicts, but also tackle, in some way or other, the ultimate relationship between literature and life, between ethical and esthetic values, between personality and art. The very spring of his literary creation shows so many contradictory elements that he is rightly considered one of the most complex and puzzling figures in European letters. In fact, it is impossible to understand

* In his letters to Pletnyov and Pogodin, after Pushkin's death.

his works unless we approach him both as man and as writer, thus combining the esthetic and the pyschological analysis. In Gogol's case, at any rate, these two kinds of criticism strengthen and complete each other.

Chapter Two

GOGOL'S FIRST STEPS IN LIFE AND IN LETTERS

I

GOGOL was a native of the Ukraine, or Little Russia. Practically the whole of this country can be described as a transition between the north and south, sometimes even as a blending of both at their best. Its population, too, bears the stamp : it combines the northern melancholy with a kind of nonchalant ease, and with a keen sense of humour. In spite of their external phlegm, the people living in this fairest part of the Russian Empire are very expansive and at times as care-free as the wind which sings over their immense landscapes. They have also preserved a certain amount of nomadic restlessness and a strong love of adventure—probably inherited from those Cossacks who once protected the banks of the Dnyeper from their ancient foes, the Turks and Tartars.

FIRST STEPS

It is almost impossible to grasp the spirit of the Ukraine apart from its old Cossack traditions. The first bands of the so-called Cossacks must have been a picturesque medley of born adventurers, naïve idealists, religious fanatics, fugitive serfs, robbers and outlaws. Their life was one of continuous daring and danger : a wild romance, gushing forth as it were from their exuberant, untamed vitality. They revelled with childlike glee in quarrels, in warfare, and often simply in robbing expeditions. But they knew how to revel in peace as well. A quiet and well-ordered existence was as foreign to their ambitions as a cage is to an eagle.

A glimpse into the way of their life can be obtained from Gogol's *Taras Bulba*—a romance full of that magic which one gets from a poetic contact with days and deeds long past. This is how he describes Syetch, the Cossack headquarters in the years of its glory :

"The whole of the Syetch presented an unusual scene. It was an unbroken revel : a ball noisily begun, which had no end. Some busied themselves with handicrafts ; others kept little shops and traded ; but the majority caroused from morning till night, if the wherewithal jingled in their pockets, and if the booty they had captured had not already passed into the hands of shop-keepers and spirit-sellers. This universal revelry had something fascinating about it. It was not an assembly of topers, who drank to drown sorrow, but simply a wild revelry of joy. Everyone who came thither forgot everything, abandoned everything which had hitherto interested him. He, so to speak, spat upon his past and gave himself recklessly up to freedom, and the good fellowship of men of the same stamp as himself—idlers having neither relatives nor home, nor family, nor anything, in short, save the free sky and the eternal revel of their souls. This gave rise to that wild gaiety which could not have sprung from any other source. The tales and talk current among the assembled crowd reposing lazily on the ground were often so droll and breathed such power of vivid narration, that it required all the nonchalance of a Cossack to retain his immovable expression, a feature which to this day distinguishes the Southern Russian from his northern brethren. It was a drunken, noisy mirth ; but there was no dark ale-house where a man drowns thought in stupefying intoxication : it was a dense throng of schoolboys.

"The only difference with regard to the students was that instead of sitting under the pointer and listening to the worn-out doctrines of a teacher, they practised racing with five thousand horses ; instead of the field where they had played ball, they had the boundless borderlands, where at the sight of them the Tartar showed his keen face and the Turk frowned grimly from under his green turban. The difference was that, instead of being forced to the companionship of school, they themselves had deserted their fathers and mothers and fled from their homes ; that here were those about whose neck a rope had already been wound, and who, instead of pale death had seen life, and life in all its intensity ; those who, from generous habits, could never keep a coin in their pockets ; those who had hitherto regarded a ducat as wealth and whose pockets, thanks to the Jew, could have been turned inside out without any danger of anything falling from them. Here were scholars who could not endure the academic rod, and had not carried away a single letter from the schools ; but with them were also some who knew about Horace, Cicero, and the Roman Republic. There were many leaders who afterwards distinguished themselves in the King's armies ; and there were numerous clever partisans who cherished a magnanimous conviction that it was of no consequence where they fought so long as they did fight, since it was a disgrace to an honourable man to live without fighting. There were many who had come to the Syetch for the sake of saying they had been there and were therefore hardened warriors. But who was not there ? This strange republic was a necessary outgrowth of the epoch. Lovers of a warlike life, of golden beakers and rich brocades, of ducats and gold pieces, could always find employment there. The lovers of women alone could find naught, for no woman dared show herself in the suburbs of Syetch."

The whole of the Ukraine is still permeated with reminiscences of the old Cossack life. Its folk-ballads, the so-called *dumy*, celebrate not mythological heroes like the Great Russian *byliny*,* but the real history turned into poetry. The innate poetical vein of the people transmuted the national past, covering it with a romantic haze and beauty. The commercial spirit of our age remained unknown to this part of the world until the second half of the last century. And even then the ravages of industrialism were limited only to certain areas, without affecting very much the delightful primitiveness of the masses.

II

Gogol's birth-place, Sorochintsy, lies near Poltava, in the central and most typical part of the Ukraine. His parents belonged to the petty

* The Ukraine became united to Russia in 1654. Its speech differs from the Great-Russian tongue considerably more than Scottish does from English proper.

land-owning nobility and claimed their descent from genuine Cossack stock. His grandfather had even been a kind of secretary in one of the Cossack regiments, and as a typical representative of the good old time, he knew many tales and anecdotes, some of which must have influenced Gogol's early works. Otherwise, the immediate ancestors of the great writer did not excel in any respect. As to his mother, she was scarcely fifteen years old when she gave birth to him, and with all her incurable enthusiasm and various slightly abnormal *idées fixes* she remained a provincial girl of fifteen till the end of her life. In her autobiographical notes she confesses with charming naïveté that at the time of getting married she was very fond of her future husband, so fond indeed that she could not find out whom she loved more—him or one of her old aunts. Apart from this, she was rather pretty, unpractical, very pious, endowed with a vivid imagination, and extremely superstitious. Gogol's father was a diseased and sentimental country squire, with a weak character but a fairly strong artistic temperament. Although ill and subject to sudden fits of hypochondria, he excelled as a humorous *conteur* and occasionally also as a good actor; he even wrote several comedies (for private performances), but like most artistic natures he was a bad manager of his own affairs. He died in 1825.

The offspring of such a couple could hardly boast of overflowing vitality, energy and health. The little Nikolai (born on 31st March, 1809) was in fact a frail child, with a rather sickly face. But for this very reason he was all the more idolized by his mother who developed an almost morbid attachment for him. He became her *enfant gâté*, whom she loved him far too much to refuse anything to him. But while gratifying all his caprices and fancies, she unwittingly encouraged in him certain features which were bound to make him later wilful and self-centred. In one of his letters Gogol says quite plainly to his mother when recollecting his childhood, " I remember : I never felt anything strongly, I looked upon all as if it were created for the purpose of gratifying me. I loved no one in particular except you, and I loved you only because Nature herself had inspired me with this feeling. I looked upon everything with dispassionate eyes : I went to the church either because I was ordered to go, or because I was carried there ; but the only thing of which I used to be aware in it were the garments of the priest and the odious howling of the sacristans. I crossed myself only because I saw other people doing the same. But once—I remember this as vividly as if it had happened just now—I asked you to tell me something about the Last Judgment, and you told me so nicely, so clearly and touchingly of those blessings of which virtuous people will partake ; you described so strikingly, in such a horrifying way, the eternal torments of the sinners that all my sentiments became awakened and almost shattered, a fact which instilled and stirred up in me, later on, the loftiest thoughts."

One can gather already from this confession that his early education was not quite reasonable or harmonious. It fostered his naïve egocentric tendency, thwarting to a certain extent the development of his spontaneous affections ; at the same time it gave an exaggerated, hyperbolical character to all those ideas and sentiments which were aroused by his own imagination. As if suspecting the coldness of his own heart, Gogol tried—even in his early years—to make up for it by the warmth of his imagination : instead of feeling genuinely, he often only imagined he felt ; and he usually took, or forced himself to take, these imaginary sentiments for real ones. This feature strikes one very unpleasantly in most of the letters he wrote to his parents from the college in Nyezhin whither he was sent after his first education at home and at Poltava. All his letters of that period are painfully rhetorical, full of melodramatic adjectives, faked emotions and false pretences, particularly where his own personal needs or achievements are concerned.

Like many exceptional men, Gogol was an exceptionally bad pupil. In the college he had acquired no serious knowledge whatever. He showed considerable zeal for literature, at least during the last two or three years of his studies in Nyezhin which he finished in 1828; yet the province in which he excelled was that of private performances in the school itself. He was particularly good at impersonating elderly and more or less comic characters. He also had some talent for painting, but none for social intercourse. Being shy and unadaptable, he was not popular among his school-fellows who called him—"the mysterious dwarf". On the other hand, he soon became dreaded by many of his comrades on account of his sharp and sarcastic tongue.

Gogol's early years at Nyezhin—the years during which he was for the first time confronted with people and conditions quite different from those in his family—must have greatly influenced the further development of his character. It is often our first steps in the world that show whether we are born to be strangers or welcome guests in this life. And in so far as the young Gogol was concerned, he certainly had few features that would entitle him to feel perfectly "at home" either with people or with life in general. He was very thin, small of stature and awkward in movements. His sickly bird-like face, too, was far from being attractive. And so after all the former adoration on the part of his mother, he soon realized that strangers were perhaps inclined to laugh at him rather than idolize him in the way he used to be idolized before. Being by nature endowed with too nervous a sensitiveness, he reacted in a passive manner : he withdrew into himself like a snail into its shell, looking with a morbid diffidence at people and things around him—always reserved, always self-conscious, and always on his guard as it were. Afraid of being laughed at, he noticed every unpleasant trifle that had the smallest relation to himself ; but out of sheer self-defence he tried at the same time to discover in other people such features as were worth laughing at : he began to ridicule, in order to save himself from being ridiculed. He developed his power of observation in a negative direction chiefly because in this way alone he could assert himself against others and emphasize his own superiority. Yet his very reserve often brought him to the other extreme : to a kind of exaggerated gaiety, familiarity, and a tendency towards reckless boyish pranks. The more inferior to others he felt in his physique and his clumsy manners, the more violently did he react by self-assertive poses, by showing off, by false pretences, as well as by a passionate ambition to achieve something that would raise him above ordinary human beings. This ambition became one of his obsessions, and it was all the more imperative the more he suffered from the awareness of his own defects and weaknesses. Another somewhat revengeful form of reaction against the feeling of his own insignificance consisted in his natural propensity to mimic and make fun of grown-ups, and particularly of old people. He often indulged in this habit, which probably helped to develop in him one of his characteristic gifts—the sense of parody and the grotesque. Together with all this he could not help feeling, even as a boy, that he *was* different from others ; yet he never could find out and express in what this difference consisted. He saw only a rapidly growing gulf between himself and the world, and the less he was able to explain it the more restless, diffident and " mysterious " he became.

It is obvious that such an inner constitution can hardly foster that natural and simple human relationship which is devoid of any second thoughts or suspicions. The spontaneous contact with other beings is made almost impossible. Any intercourse with them becomes at last a burden. And so the self-centred individual retires into his own ego, into those subjective fancies and illusions which are likely to give an imaginary compensation for all that he lacks. This attitude towards external life is bound to affect his imagination by developing it out of all proportion to his other qualities. So much so that eventually he exaggerates everything he sees, thinks, feels ; everything that he expects or wishes to happen. The usual result is a kind of continuous dismay at the difference between the actual facts and his own exalted anticipations. With the years he thus becomes utterly incapable of enjoying reality and loses all inner touch with it owing precisely to his vivid imagination which always promises more than life can give, and therefore always deceives him. His artificial exaltation soon gives way to disappointment, to despondence and pessimism. Reality begins to appear as a hostile agency which must be exposed, rejected. The weaker he feels in the face of this agency the greater his pleasure in denouncing all its negative and vulnerable points. Whenever he leaves his own " romantic " world of fancies, he usually does so in order to find a few more proofs that the actual world which has rejected him deserves to be rejected *by him*. It is here that his observing capacities assume a morbid and one-sided direction, while the growing occupation with his own moods may increase his egotism up to the point of exalted vanity and monomania.*

* This vanity can often assume the mark of saintliness or moral superiority. But that makes it only more interesting to a psychological observer.

Such extremes were typical of Gogol already in his boyhood. Like all introvert characters, he was always inclined to underrate himself. But out of the sheer instinct of inner self-preservation he reacted to the opposite state of mind: to vanity and conceit. He began to cling to every illusion which promised to emphasize the importance of his own ego. Even in those early years he indulged in self-praise and in a kind of irresponsible Tarasconism whenever his own person was in question. Carried away by this he was prone to romance about himself to such an extent as to obliterate the line between truth and mystification. This continuous wavering between the two opposite impulses and tendencies is very well illustrated by Gogol's early letters, above all by those he wrote during his school years (from 1820 to 1828): they are as puzzling, contradictory and chaotic as his entire personality. Apart from the already mentioned "faked" feelings, they often bewilder us by the amount of incongruities one finds in them. They show us a boy who is lyrical and reflective, naïve and cunning, melancholy and full of gaiety, insinuating and conceited, didactic and self-accusing, pious and yet often hypocritical, affectionate and "practical" (particularly when he wants to get more money out of his parents), lonely, sentimental, doubting his own strength, curiously restless, and all the time digging into his own self. He is too reserved to be entirely open about his real feelings, and at the same time too scrupulous to be entirely insincere. And the more he suspects his lack of sincerity the more he tries to mask it from himself and from others by a kind of rhetorical and melodramatic exuberance, which strikes one so unpleasantly even in the letter he wrote to his mother on his father's death.

He himself early became conscious of all the complexity of his nature, and he suffered from the chaos of his inner contradictions without being able to alter it. He was all the more perplexed by it because he realized that behind his external masks there was, nevertheless, an ardent soul distorted through its own loneliness, diffidence and reserve. "I often wondered how it is that God has created a unique and rare heart, a soul which is full of ardent love for all that is lofty and beautiful—and why has He enveloped all this in such a rough exterior?" he complains to his mother in 1829. "Why has He combined all this with such a terrible mixture of contradictions, obstinacy, insolent conceit and base humility? But my perishable mind is not strong enough to fathom the great designs of the Almighty." And in another letter (December 20th, 1827) he says again:

" Truly, I am considered a puzzle by all, but no one has unravelled me completely. At home they take me for an obstinate fellow—for a kind of unbearable pundit who deems himself cleverer than the rest of the world and different from other human beings. Will you believe me that inwardly I have laughed, together with you, over all this ? Here, on the contrary, I am called a humble spirit, a paragon of modesty and patience. In one place I am in fact the quietest, the most unassuming and polite person, in another—sullen, brooding, awkward, etc : and in a third again—a chatterbox and a regular nuisance ; with some people I am clever, with others stupid. Do think of me as you like, but it is only my real life-work that will reveal to you also my real character."

The problem of such " real life-work " began to trouble Gogol's mind very early indeed. The strange point, however, is that his ambitions of those days were not literary at all. His favourite dream was to become a great dignitary and statesman. This dream was probably fostered by the pomp and magnificence he had often witnessed as a boy on the estate of his distant relation, Troschinsky—a former minister and retired potentate who was fond of displaying, in a theatrical way, all his wealth and self-importance. Yet it would be wrong to see in

Gogol's plans only a desire to distinguish himself above others, and to prove that he was not as insignificant as he looked. At the bottom of his ambitions there certainly was this impulse, but it was always mixed with elements of a different and higher kind : with genuine idealism ; with a sound craving for self-realization on such a big scale as to be worth while ; and above all with an almost panic fear of seeing his own life wasted on vulgar trifles—wasted in the same senseless manner as the majority of human lives. This is what he wrote, towards the end of his studies, to his friend Vysotsky who was at that time (26th October, 1827) in Petersburg : " I don't know whether my plans will come true—whether I, too, shall live in that heavenly spot [*i.e.*, Petersburg] or whether the wheel of fate will cruelly fling me, together with the crowds of self-contented mob—what a terrible thought !—into the realm of nobodies, consigning me to the gloomy quarter of obscurity." Or take this passage to his uncle Kossyarovsky (October 3rd, 1827) : " Cold sweat pours down my face at the idea that I shall perhaps perish in dust, without making my name known by a single remarkable deed—to live in this world without making my existence worth while would be terrible." And he adds, " I have meditated upon all careers and state-offices, and I have decided to take up jurisprudence. I see that here there is more work to be done than anywhere else, and that here alone I can be a real benefactor to humanity."

III

It was with this aim that the young Gogol left for Petersburg. But his expectations met here with cruel blows. The " heavenly spot " of his letters soon proved to be more like a hell for a man without money and without connections. Instead of being welcomed by all and sundry, he discovered that in the capital he was of hardly more account than a stray cat or a mouse. Instead of renting a palace on the Neva embankment, he had to content himself with humble fifth-floor rooms in one of the side-streets. And instead of a brilliant career in which he could shower blessings upon humanity, he vainly sought the post of an underpaid clerk. He tried his luck also as an actor, but during the test his voice proved so weak that he had to part with this illusion as well.

After such failures he decided to embark upon a literary adventure. He happened to bring in his luggage a sentimental idyll in verse, written by him probably in the college. Its theme was taken from German life. Its title, too, was

German (*Hans Küchelgarten*) and so was its chief source of inspiration—the poet Voss, whose *Luise* Gogol must have known both from the original and from a Russian translation. Yet the theme itself is characteristic of the young Gogol in so far as it deals with the conflict between the craving for a happy existence, rooted in the idyllic native soil, and the desire to tear oneself away from it in order to roam about and shape one's own destiny in the *grand monde*. The restless Hans leaves his snug home, his betrothed, his country ; but after all his wanderings and experiences in the world he returns tired and disappointed, marries his pretty Louise and probably lives happy ever after. Apart from a certain bearing upon the author himself, Gogol's idyll is on the whole uninteresting, poor and conventional. Its language, its rhythm and rhymes are conspicuous chiefly by their lack of craft and inspiration. Nothing, except perhaps a couple of descriptive passages, shows that this feeble work had been written by a man of promise. Nevertheless Gogol was imprudent enough to publish it—under an assumed name (Alov) and at his own expense. The result can be imagined. The author was so shocked by the slighting reviews on the part of those few critics who had deigned to take notice of his literary production that he collected all the remaining copies and burned them. Depressed by his ill-luck, by destitution, as well as by complete uncertainty with regard to his future, he decided at last to leave Russia.

Perhaps he had a real intention of starting a career abroad, above all in America. On the other hand, after many blows and blunders in the Russian capital, he most probably wanted just to escape, no matter where—in order to forget all about it. Be this as it may, the fact is that one fine day he appropriated a sum of money belonging to his mother, went aboard the first foreign ship he could find and sailed to Germany. He stopped for three days in Lübeck, and went to one or two other places, but deceived once more in his romantic anticipations (and also by his funds), he soon returned to Petersburg. The motives with which he tried to explain his escapade in the letters to his mother were both cunning and naïve. Now he wished to justify it by some illness in his chest from which he wanted to find a cure abroad, then by the mighty will of God Himself, or even by his incurable love for a woman. This woman existed, of course, in his imagination only. Yet it is quite possible that he himself believed in the truth of these flowery passages which he wrote home almost on the eve of his queer journey (July 27th, 1824) : " To you alone I can tell all about it . . . You know that I have always been endowed with such firmness as is rarely to be found in a young man . . . Who could have expected a weakness of this kind on my part? But I saw her . . . No, I will not tell her name . . . She is too exalted for anyone, not only for me . . . No, this was not love . . . At any rate, I have never heard of a similar love. In a fit of madness and of terrible inner torments I was craving, I was burning to get intoxicated by a single look of hers."

Meanwhile, his external life did not show much improvement. On his return from Lübeck he obtained a very insignificant post in one of the Government Offices. He is even supposed to have served for a while in the notorious "Third Department. However, this supposition, which is based chiefly on the questionable evidence of Bulgarin, is still much in the dark.* Even if the unpractical Gogol had taken—as his last resort—a post in that department, he must have left it very soon.

It was about that time that Gogol tried again his luck in literature. Seeing that various ethnographic motives, particularly those of Little

* The so-called Third Department was created by Nicholas I with the special purpose of spying upon the liberals and revolutionaries. Bulgarin's incrimination with regard to Gogol can be found in *The Northern Bee* of 1854, No. 175.

Russia, were the literary fashion of the day, he began to write on Ukrainian subjects, published some of his articles and narrative fragments in the press, and even managed to come into touch with Zhukovsky, with Professor Pletnyov, and later on (1831) with Pushkin. It was probably in 1830 that he met also the brilliant lady-in-waiting, Mlle Rosset,* a great friend of literature, and even more of *littérateurs*, to many of whom she rendered such valuable services in mitigating the severity of the censors, that she was nicknamed *Notre Dame de bon secours de la littérature russe en détresse*. Owing to Pletnyov's protection, Gogol obtained the post of teacher at the "Patriotic Institute". But here, too, he was so badly paid that he had to eke out his living by private lessons. Count V. A. Sollogub relates in his *Reminiscences* how he met Gogol in 1831, when the future great writer was engaged as tutor to a half-witted son of Sollogub's aunt in Pavlovsk. "We entered the nursery," he says "where at the writing table the teacher sat; he was showing to his pupil pictures of various animals, imitating at the same time their bleating, bellowing, grunting, etc., 'This one, darling, is a ram; do you follow? A ram—be, be. . . . This here is a cow, you know, a cow, moo, moo . . . .' And the tutor went on imitating their

* Later Mme. Smirnova.

sounds with a queer, peculiar pleasure. I confess that I felt sad when looking upon such a scene—upon the pitiable lot of a man compelled to do this kind of work in order to earn his daily bread. I quickly left the room, hardly paying any attention to the voice of my aunt who introduced the teacher to me by his full name : Nikolai Vassilyevitch Gogol."

The endless drudgery of the first few months that followed on Gogol's return from abroad, the damp and foggy climate, the dreary existence devoid of prospects, all this threatened to crush the nervous and unbalanced youth. But here his own imagination came to his rescue. He began to fight his depression by conjuring up the brightest pictures, tales and traditions of his sunny Ukraine. In fancy, at any rate, he returned to his native soil (like his vagrant Hans), and he revelled, he bathed in it. In the glowing images of the south-Russian peasant life, of their mirth and laughter, he forgot for a while the drab reality he had to endure. This is how he wrote most of the stories which were published under the title, *The Evenings on a Farm near Dikanka* (the first volume in 1831, and the second in the following year).

These stories were the first spontaneous flower of Gogol's genius. At one stroke, and almost by chance, he discovered his real vocation. He was like a weary traveller who sits down on the ground and finds there a gold mine. Owing to their atmosphere of romance and folklore, *The Evenings* certainly did respond to the demand of the day, but they did so in a profoundly original and unique manner. One could point to a number of other writers who had used similar subjects before Gogol, and yet none of their works would stand comparison with his achievement. Even now, almost a hundred years after their publication, these stories have not lost an ounce of their inimitable charm and freshness. They still infect us with their fragrance and gaiety, their boisterous humour, colour and music. Bielinsky, the most influential critic of that period, hailed them with enthusiasm and summed up (in 1835) his final verdict in these words : " All that is beautiful in nature, all that fascinates us in the rural life of the simple folk, all that is typical and original in it, glitters like a rainbow in these first poetic fancies of Gogol. This was a youthful poesy, fresh, fragrant, gorgeous and intoxicating like the kiss of love. Read his *May Night*, read it on a winter evening by the blazing hearth, and you will forget all about the winter with its frosts and storms. You will see in your mind the brilliant clear night of the blissful south ; you will see the pale young heroine —the victim of an evil stepmother's fury, the lonely dwelling with one window open, the deserted lake and its still waters on which the moonbeams are playing ; while on its green banks whirl hosts of aerial beauties . . . This impression is similar to that which Shakespeare's *Midsummer Night's Dream* leaves in one's imagination." And again : " Each period of human life is beautiful and must have its songs and singers. *The Evenings on a Farm* is one of such eternal songs of youth—a song which brings back for a moment, even to our old age, all the enchantment of those young years that are irrevocably gone."

IV

Each part of *The Evenings* includes four stories. In the first volume we find, *The Fair of Sorochintsy*, *St. John's Eve*, *The May Night*, *The Lost Letter ;* and in the second, *The Christmas Eve*, *The Cruel Vengeance*, *Ivan Shponka and his Aunt*, and *The Bewitched Spot.*

The feature which strikes one at the very first perusal of these fancies is their lack of literary conventions. One feels that Gogol wrote them not in order to imitate anyone but just to suit his own whims and inclinations—to be himself, in short. That is why there is a charm of wild flowers about them. Unhampered by any literary cultor "culture", Gogol was free to follow his own inspiration, which always prompted the right thing, whether it were a lyrical passage, a romantic whim, a farcical situation brimming with humour, or a grotesque mixture of the real world with the world of fancy—taken from Ukrainian folk-lore. There is only one story in the *Evenings* which is entirely free from folk-lore elements, *Ivan Shponka and his Aunt*, but it is of interest that it remained unfinished like his earlier sketch of the same grotesquely "realistic" kind—*The Fearful Boar* (*Strashny Kaban*). The arbitrary mixture of the actual world with the world of ghosts and goblins was apparently more to the taste of the youthful author ; for it always made him create a reality of his own in which these two worlds could blend—a reality in which he was absolute master and ruler, free from any imperatives of that matter-of-fact existence which he wanted to forget. But in spite of all this, Gogol rarely *invents* anything except the setting. His imagination is not inventive at all, but intensifying ; and this is of great importance. For whereas the purely inventive kind of imagination can always be self-supporting, the intensifying one leans upon some given data which it selects, re-arranges, often distorts, and then combines in its own way. Gogol's imagination is almost entirely of the second kind. Hence, instead of inventing his own themes and their details, he *collects* them : he takes them either from real anecdotes, from reminiscences of his childhood, from folk-tales, from private information,* or even from his father's comedies. But once having collected the necessary elements he modifies them, rearranges their proportions, and by the sheer heat of his artistic gift he blends them into perfect works of art.

True, this *intensifying* kind of fancy may run a great danger ; for if applied to certain aspects of everyday life, it may exaggerate, magnify and distort them so much as to convert every trifle into a kind of haunting spook which threatens to disturb one's inner balance. It is significant that Gogol's own imagination did develop in this sense. Deeply rooted in his inherited hypochondria, it often made him indulge both in morbid exaggerations and morbid superstitions. Many years later, at the age of forty, he wrote : " Everything is disorganized within me. I see, for example, that somebody has stumbled ; my imagination immediately gets hold of it, begins to develop it into the shape of most horrid apparitions which torture me so much

* While writing his first stories, and also his later work, Gogol often entreated his mother to send him information concerning Ukrainian peasant life, folk-lore, etc.

that I cannot sleep and am losing all my strength."

But this is only the pathologic aspect of that very quality which helped him to write magnificent things as long as he was able to sublimate it through art. And his *Evenings* certainly is one of the most delightful sublimations of this kind. Take its very first few pages. The whole story under the title, *The Fair of Sorochintsy*, is just an ordinary anecdote about a pig-headed peasant who is fooled by the lad to whom he does not want to give his daughter in marriage. Gogol extends this anecdote into a thrilling buffoonery in which a whole country fair takes part, the action moving rapidly as in a cinema until it reaches its acme of fun and finishes favourably not only for the enamoured couple, but also for the gipsy who plays the part of bribed providence. In *St. John's Eve* again Gogol slightly reminds us of Tieck's *Liebeszauber*, yet its setting, its style and tone are thoroughly original. Or take his *Christmas Eve* in which village lads, drunkards, worthies and witches, Cossacks and devils are mixed with each other as in a gay kaleidoscope. This story, too is based upon a ready-made anecdote : an Ukrainian tale about the devil who wished to ruin a pious blacksmith and was himself pulled by the nose instead. In Gogol's version the crafty blacksmith, Vakula, compels the devil to carry him, on the very eve of Christmas, to Petersburg, where he joins a deputation of Cossacks paying homage to Catharine II ; but having obtained the golden slippers from the Empress herself he hurries back, carried again by the devil, and gives them to his proud Oksana whose heart naturally softens after such a feat. Also the *Lost Letter* and *The Bewitched Spot* are anecdotes which Gogol must have heard either from his grandfather, or from some other old Cossack. To put it briefly, Gogol's themes are hardly ever his own ; he picks them up where he can. But this raw material he transforms into real works of art, every line of which seems to be seething with his own verve, with the delightful pranks of his fancy, with lyrical intermezzos, unexpected metaphors, humorous allusions, gestures and grimaces—as if retold or improvized by a matchless impersonator.

One cannot help wondering at the number of various elements which Gogol binds together and blends in perfect harmony. The sentimental-romantic motives are mingled with the funniest situations imaginable ; the gruesome *Cruel Vengeance* is followed by tales of a farcical nature ; and even in one and the same story the whimsical tone of the author often gives way to sudden lyrical passages of great beauty, especially when he describes his native south. Sometimes one almost feels a hidden antagonism between the descriptive and the narrative elements, between the born *painter* and the born *actor*, in Gogol. But again his pictures, particularly those of nature, are never realistic, although they are pieced together from entirely realistic details. Many of his descriptions of scenery—for instance that of the Ukrainian May night, or of the Dnyeper—have become classic. Yet it is enough to read them carefully in order to find out that they are in essence as artificial as the scenery in an opera or a ballet. They are too subjective to have anything in common with real nature. Gogol borrows from it colours, trees, steppes, stars and rivers, yet he can visualize only that landscape which he himself has constructed in accordance with his own moods, needs, fancies and visions. He feels and sees in fact only that nature which is in his own imagination and not in reality. He also makes a much too frequent use of hyperbolism. So much so that his epithets are sometimes dangerously near the line of abstract *clichés*. And yet there *is* beauty in all that—not only descriptive, but above all lyrical and musical beauty. For Gogol has an almost astonishing sense for the magic of words and sounds as such, quite apart from their actual meaning. He feels the " aura " of every word, he revels in verbal accords, in rhythms and intonations to such an extent as to saturate every sentence with musical content. It is for musical reasons that he often piles period upon period, picture upon picture, each more glowing than the last, until he comes to the verge of rhetoric. Take this opening of the *Fair of Sorochintsy*.

" How gorgeous, how intoxicating is a summer day in Little Russia ! How languidly hot are the hours when the noon glitters in its sweat and silence, and when the blue immeasurable vault of heaven, bent over the world like a voluptuous cupola, seems to have fallen asleep, bathing in a sea of rapture—while holding and caressing the beautiful earth in its ethereal embraces. Not a cloud in the sky, not a sound in the fields. All is silent as if dead ; only there, in the heavenly heights, a lark trembles, and silvery songs float on airy waves to the enchanted earth below ; now and then the call of a gull is heard, or the resonant voice of a quail echoes in the steppe. Lazily and lost in dreams like aimless wanderers stand the cloud-high oaks, and the blinding beats of sun rays light up masses of leaves, while on others they cast a shade dark as night and yet sprinkled with gold at every gush of the breeze. Emeralds, topazes, jacinths of ethereal insects are pouring over the gay-coloured gardens protected by stately sun-flowers. Grey stacks of hay and golden sheaves of corn seem to be camping in the field over all its boundless expanse. The verdant branches of cherry, apple, pear and plum-trees, bent by the weight of their fruits ; the sky and its clear mirror—the river framed in the green, proudly elevated banks . . . How luxurious, how voluptuous is the Ukrainian summer ! "

V

The intensity of Gogol's early stories is due to two reasons : one of them is that he wrote them as an antidote against his own depression ; and the other—the intimate connection with his soil and race.

" The cause of that gaiety which one had noticed in my first works was a kind of inner need," Gogol confessed much later. " I became a prey to fits of melancholy which were beyond my comprehension . . . In order to get rid of them I invented the funniest things I could think of. I invented funny characters in the funniest situations imaginable."

This kind of artistic creation, that is, creation as the result of an inner conflict with oneself and with reality, must have a certain influence upon one's style. A quiet classic style is here out of the question, since one's urgent personal need always increases the personal note. And this we feel distinctly in Gogol's prose. However deliberately and calmly he may have collected single ingredients of his stories, during the process of creation he gets carried away—not so much by the literary as by the musical side of words and phrases. Hence his nervous exuberance, his rhythmic cadences, blazing flashes of colour, numerous adjectives and waving periods full of unexpected similes, metaphors and idioms which make one think that Gogol probably wanted to forget himself in all this as in a dancing whirl.

But let us turn to the racial element in Gogol's writings. It would be highly interesting to explore the proportion between the racial and the individual elements in the consciousness of a genius, but this is beyond the scope of the present work. Suffice it to say that the artistic power of a great writer is often due to his being "rooted" in his own race, from which he draws a continuous supply of mental energy. True, this bond is entirely subconscious and in most cases atavistic; yet it can become a great creative agent. A careful reader of Gogol, Dostoevsky and Tolstoy, for example, can easily perceive with his "second sight" how much they gain from the *organic* nearness to their own racial collective—a nearness which is impossible in more civilized and therefore more disintegrated communities. The influence of this bond may be sometimes so strong as to urge one back to primitive masses and deny all individualization whatsoever.*

Gogol, in particular, is one of the few European writers who could create occasionally by being in tune as it were with the folk-genius and taking from its treasury all he needed. However lonely and *déraciné* he might have felt in the official world of Petersburg, the deeper layers of his soul were still linked to the patriarchal and almost mythological spirit of his race. His mentality was in fact nearer to the realm of mythology than to that of literature proper. It was not literary culture, of which Gogol had practically none, that carried him through, but an instinct akin to that which is at the bottom of folk-art. For, although not "inventive" in itself, the young Gogol's imagination retained that kind of vision which is largely on the plane of peasant art, of mythology and poetic superstition. The devil himself seems to have the same undeniable reality to him as to a simple Ukrainian peasant. And however humorously he may treat various demonic agencies, at bottom he still believes in them, feels their mysterious influence upon life, and is even afraid of them.

* Tolstoy's "Christian" communism was largely a disguised impulse of this kind.

His theme is often that of the *dumy* (in his *Cruel Vengeance*, for example), and his gaiety that of the popular *vertep* : the Ukrainian Punch-and-Judy show. Many of Gogol's figures and situations were modelled on the farcical traditional types of the *vertep*-interludes, which comprised among its marionettes the brave Cossack, the boasting Pole, the comic Jew, the ubiquitous devil, the sly *dyachok* (scribe), and the dexterous bursar or divinity student.* All these figures we meet, under some disguise or other, in Gogol's early stories ; and in a way they are as stereotyped as those of folk-tales and folk-ballads : with no deliberate psychology, no inner life, no ethical criticism or censure of their actions. Gogol is here as little " realistic " as the weavers of the wonderful patterns which we find in old tapestries. And his humour too is that of the *vertep*—the humour of situations, not of characters ; so are his names, such as Golopupenko, Sverbygooz, etc., names which are entirely untranslatable in their comic, even obscenely-comic aspect.

And so, in spite of his " collecting " method, Gogol's *Evenings on a Farm* are a fine example of individual productions on the plane of racial

* It is noteworthy that one of Gogol's ancestors, a certain Tansky (died in 1763) had written several comic interludes in Little Russian.

genius and folk-lore. One is almost tempted to call them intensified folk-tales. Anyhow, Gogol is here unique, largely by coming so near to the folk-tone and by being so racial. His very language is new and unique : the powerful great-Russian tongue, enriched by all the music and feminine plasticity of its southern sister. For this reason Gogol's works can be really appreciated only in the original. Even the best foreign versions compare with it in the same way as artificial flowers would compare with those in the fields. Besides, it is only second-rate poets and writers that translate well. A great artist is untranslatable. And Gogol is the least translatable of all Russian writers.

Chapter Three

THE INVERTED ROMANTICIST

I

GOGOL was probably himself surprised by the unexpected success of his first stories. This surprise must have been all the more welcomed by him because of his previous doubts and disappointments. Here was at last a tangible proof that fate had not relegated him to the " dark quarter of obscurity ". But as though not quite sure of his own achievement, he began to magnify its significance, showing off, posing and indulging in conceit. He instinctively tried to cope with his lack of confidence by a kind of exaggerated self-assurance and self-importance coupled with naïve vanity. Sometimes, at any rate, he behaved like a *nouveau riche* from the provinces. So much so that even those who admired his talent were hardly inclined to admire his manners.

An account of what he was like after his brilliant début is given by S. T. Aksakov, the well-known author of the *Family Chronicle*. This good-natured Russian *barin* made Gogol's acquaintance in 1832 in Moscow, and he describes him as follows : " The external appearance of Gogol was not in his favour at that time ; a crest of hair on his head, carefully clipped kiss-curls on his temples, clean-shaven lips and chin, and an enormous over-starched collar gave an artificial expression to his face ; there seemed to be in him something crested and cunning. In his costume pretentions to dandyism were noticeable. I remember he had a bright motley waistcoat with a big watch-chain. On the whole, there was something in him which restrained me from any sincere enthusiasm and warmth, in which I so often indulge. At his request, I took him to Zagoskin. On the way Gogol surprised me by complaining about his own diseases and even said he was incurably ill. As he seemed to be in perfect health I looked at him with wondering and incredulous eyes. 'What is wrong with you?' I asked. He answered vaguely that the cause of his ailment was in his intestines." Aksakov quotes also his son's * remarks about the painful impression produced on all by the young Gogol

* Konstantine Aksakov, who became afterwards a famous Slavophile, *i.e.*, one of the champions of the national Russian culture and institutions, as opposed to those of the European West.

who "behaved rudely, negligently, and looked upon people from above, as it were."

The first few years of Gogol's fame were nevertheless unsettled, both materially and otherwise. Owing to various influences, he obtained, in 1834, the chair of History in Petersburg University, although he had never had an opportunity of acquiring any serious knowledge of the subject. As he had no scientific training nor any regard for mental discipline, he naturally clung to a romantic conception of history with a comfortable belief in Providence, with a kind of hero-worship, and with boundless admiration for the feudal Middle Ages. He ignored all epochs of human history except the Middle Ages on the one hand, and the picturesque Cossack-period of his native Ukraine on the other. The Greeks and Romans simply did not exist for him.

It is obvious that this new career of Gogol could not be exactly brilliant. The flashing success of his first lecture, on the Middle Ages, was due to his artistic and in no way to his scientific equipment. But no sooner had his initial enthusiasm begun to flag than he lost all interest in lecturing. He bored his students, and the students bored him. The great novelist, Ivan Turgenev, has left this interesting account of Gogol's so-called professorship :

GOGOL

" I was one of his students in 1835, when he was lecturing (!) on history at the University of Petersburg. To tell the truth, this lecturing of his was rather queer. First of all, out of three lectures Gogol invariably missed two ; and secondly, even when he appeared in the hall, he did not talk : he only whispered incoherently about something or other, showing us little steel engravings with views of Palestine and other eastern countries. He was continuously in terrible confusion. We all were convinced (and we were hardly wrong) that he did not know anything about history, and that our professor, Gogol-Yanovsky,* had nothing in common with the writer Gogol who was then already famous by his *Evenings on a Farm near Dikanka*. At the final examination on his subject he sat, with a handkerchief wrapped round his head, simulating toothache. There was an expression of extreme pain on his face, and he never opened his mouth. Professor T. P. Shulgin examined the students for him. I see, as if it were now, Gogol's lean figure, with a long nose and the two ends of his black handkerchief surging above his head like two ears. There is no doubt that he himself understood all the comic awkwardness of his

* This second Polish name, which Gogol later abolished, was added to the original name of his parents in honour of his great-grandfather, Jan, who had become a Polish nobleman.

position, for he retired in the same year. And yet this did not prevent him from exclaiming : 'Unrecognized I took the chair, and unrecognized I leave it '."

Fortunately, he soon gave up his professorial ambitions and returned to literature as his sole vocation.

II

In the first three years following the *Evenings* Gogol seemed to have become a prey to a kind of working fever. As if afraid that his inspiration might soon desert him, he wrote with burning impatience. It was between 1832 and 1836 that he conceived practically all his works. In the same year as he left the University (1835) he published the first part of his *Mirgorod*, which includes two literary masterpieces : *The Old-World Landowners*, and *Taras Bulba*. This was soon followed by a second volume under the same title, with two more stories : *Viy* and *The Story of the Quarrel between Ivan Ivanovitch and Ivan Nikiforovitch.*

On the title page, Gogol says that these stories are a continuation of the *Evenings*. So they are in a way ; but at the same time they mark also a further development of Gogol's talent in so far as he found in them a perfect expression for his romantic temper on the one hand, and for his observation of typical details on the other. *Taras Bulba*, for instance, is the highwater mark of Gogol's romantic vein, while his *Old World Landowners* and his story of the two quarrelling Ivans consist of realistic elements only, which are " collected " and used by Gogol in quite a peculiar manner.

Being unable to adapt himself to actual life and actual surroundings, he had one alternative left : either to escape from them into the romantic atmosphere of his childhood, into his own legendary Ukraine ; or to describe them in such a way as to *expose* the given reality, to take revenge upon it by proving that it is unworthy of existence. And the more he wanted to prove this, the more realistic the data he accumulated with which to show that he was right in refuting it. Psychologically, Gogol's " realism " thus became a kind of *inverted romanticism*. Yet such a negation of the hateful present may look for comfort not only in the past, but also in the future—in a vision of life and man as they should be. Gogol was not a stranger to this impulse either ; but while a refuge in the past appealed to his romantic-esthetic temper, his preoccupation with life as it ought to be was entirely a matter of his moral and ethical instincts which eventually began to assert themselves on their own account—even against Gogol the artist.

This dilemma arose in him, however, considerably later. In the *Evenings* for example, we do not feel it at all. But in the *Mirgorod* it is perhaps slightly indicated only by certain moods which seem to go hand in hand with the growing differentiation between the romantic and the "realistic" strains in Gogol. And yet, how well he still blends the two in such a piece as *The Old-World Landowners!* On the surface this story seems to be entirely realistic—in the sense of descriptive realism. Nevertheless, all its details are so carefully chosen and constructed as to produce a thoroughly sentimental-romantic atmosphere. Its very opening shows the dominant mood and motive of the story:

"I am very fond of the modest life of those isolated owners of distant villages, which are usually called 'old-fashioned' in Little Russia, and which, like ruinous and picturesque houses, are beautiful through their simplicity and complete contrast to a new, regular building, whose walls the rain has never yet washed, whose roof is not yet covered with mould, and whose porch, undeprived of its stucco, does not yet show its red bricks. I love to enter now and then for a moment the sphere of this unusually isolated existence where no wish flies beyond the palings of the little yard, and the hedge of the garden filled with apple and plum trees ; beyond the neighbouring peasant huts, leaning on one side and shaded by willows, elder-bushes, and pear-trees. The life of the modest owners is quiet, so quiet that you forget yourself for a while, and think that the passions, wishes and the ceaseless doings of the Evil One, which keep the world in an uproar, simply don't exist, and that you had only beheld them in an exciting, dazzling dream. I can see now the low-roofed little house, with its veranda of slender, blackened tree-trunks surrounding it on all sides so that in case of a thunder or hail storm, the window shutters could be closed without your getting wet ; behind it I see fragrant wild-cherry bushes, whole rows of small fruit-trees, laden with purple cherries and with an ocean of dark-blue plums ; I see luxuriant maples, under the shade of which rugs are spread for repose, and in front of the house the spacious yard, with short, fresh grass, through which paths had been trodden from the store-houses to the kitchen, from the kitchen to the living rooms ; a long-necked goose drinking water, with her young goslings, soft as down ; the picket-fence hung with bunches of dried pears and apples, and rugs put out to air ; a cart full of melons standing near the store-house ; the unyoked ox lazily lying beside it. All this has for me an indescribable charm, perhaps because it is far away and because anything from which we are separated is pleasing to us."

Gogol here goes back to the sunny Ukraine of his childhood. He bathes, as it were, in his own reminiscences of that idyllic and almost vegetative happiness which is represented by the patriarchal owners of the low-roofed little house: the good-natured Afanasy Ivanovitch and his priceless Pulkheria Ivanovna—a kind of Ukrainian Philemon and Baucis. These two human beings, in whom Gogol is supposed to have depicted his own grandparents, have become in fact a part of Nature herself. They have eliminated all wishes that fly beyond the garden hedge, all interests that go beyond eating, sleeping and looking after their own estate. And yet this narrow life of theirs does not offend us. We accept them as they are and find a certain charm even in their gluttony. For "Afanasy Ivanovitch and Pulkheria Ivanovna, following the custom of old-fashioned gentle-folk, were very fond of eating. With the first glimmer of dawn (they got up very early) the morning coffee was on the table and they drank it to the accompaniment of the creaking of doors and the bustle of the morning housework. Having finished his coffee, Afanasy Ivanovitch would go to the hall and drive the geese out into the yard, shaking his handkerchief at them and calling 'Shoo-shoo—be off with you!' In the yard he met his bailiff and a long conversation ensued during which he showed extraordinary knowledge of the management of his estate, and his comments and orders were such that a novice would hardly have been encouraged to try and cheat him of a penny. But his bailiff was an old hand and knew well how to answer him and still better how to conduct his own affairs. The conversation over, Afanasy Ivanovitch would go back to the house and address Pulkheria Ivanovna with the words: 'Don't you think, Pulkheria Ivanovna, that it is time to have something to eat?'

" 'And what would you like to have, Afanasy Ivanovitch? Pastries with poppy seeds, or perhaps some preserved mushrooms?'

" 'Well, I don't really mind. Either pastries or mushrooms would do,' said Afanasy Ivanovitch, and as if by magic the table was laid and he sat down to eat.

"An hour before dinner Afanasy Ivanovitch partook of some vodka in an old fashioned, silver tankard and more food, such as mushrooms, salted fish, etc. They had dinner at mid-day. In addition to the plates and tureens there were a number of pots on the table from which the lids were not removed, in order to preserve the flavour of the dishes. During dinner the conversation touched on topics closely connected with the meal.

" 'It seems to me, Pulkheria Ivanovna, that this kasha is a little burned ?' Afanasy Ivanovitch would say : 'Do you notice it ?'

" 'Oh, no, Afanasy Ivanovitch. Take a little more butter or some of this mushroom sauce. Then you will see that you are mistaken.'

" 'Well, I'll try,' Afanasy Ivanovitch would answer, holding out his plate. 'We'll see how it will do.'

"Dinner over Afanasy Ivanovitch had an hour's rest, after which Pulkheria Ivanovna would bring in a sliced water-melon and say : 'Just try this lovely melon, Afanasy Ivanovitch.'

" 'Don't you be too sure that it is lovely, Pulkheria Ivanovna,' Afanasy Ivanovitch would say, taking a good slice. 'It may not be good even though it is red.' But the water-melon soon disappeared, and after eating a pear or two Afanasy Ivanovitch would go for a stroll in the garden accompanied by Pulkheria Ivanovna. When they got back to the house domestic duties claimed Pulkheria Ivanovna ; and he would sit down on the steps under an awning facing the yard and watch the maids carrying endless wooden boxes and baskets in and out of the store house. Almost at once he would send one of the maids for Pulkheria Ivanovna or would go to her himself with the question, ‘ What do you suggest that I should have to eat, Pulkheria Ivanovna ? ’

“ ‘ Now what would you like, Afanasy Ivanovitch ? Shall I ask them to bring you some of that fruit pudding which I told them to keep specially for you ? ’

“ ‘ That's a good idea.’

“ ‘ Or perhaps you would like some jelly ? ’

“ ‘ Well, that would be nice, too,’ Afanasy Ivanovitch would reply, and the food was at once brought and eaten.

“ ‘ Before supper Afanasy Ivanovitch usually had something else to eat. They supped at half past nine and went to bed directly after, when silence reigned over this active yet peaceful abode. The room in which Afanasy Ivanovitch and Pulkheria Ivanovna slept was so hot that few people could have remained there for more than an hour at a time. Afanasy Ivanovitch however, in spite of this, liked to be even warmer and slept on the bench above the stove though the heat was so unbearable that he had to get up several times in the night and walk about the room. Sometimes he would groan a little as he paced up and down and then Pulkheria Ivanovna would ask him : “ What is the matter, Afanasy Ivanovitch ? ’

“ ‘ God only knows, Pulkheria Ivanovna. I seem to have a slight stomach-ache,’ Afanasy Ivanovitch would reply.

" 'Perhaps you would feel better if you had something to eat?'

' 'I really don't know whether it would be wise, Pulkheria Ivanovna. But what do you suggest that I should have?'

" 'Would you fancy a little junket, or pears in fruit jelly?'

" 'Well, I might try just a little.'

" At this decision a sleepy maid was despatched to scour the pantry, and Afanasy Ivanovitch indulged in light refreshment after which he generally said: 'Yes, now I feel a little better.' '

The happiness of this old couple is due to a lowered consciousness, a fact which in itself is degrading. Nevertheless, owing to Gogol's warm intimate tone mixed with a mild humour we get fond of these two human beings. We enter into all the details of their unsophisticated life, their meals, their petty worries, as if they were our nearest friends. And how sorry we are for the poor Afanasy when death tears away from him his wonderful Pulkheria whom, from sheer grief, he soon follows.

The whole work is not a story proper, but a mosaic in which all trifles blend into a picture half-amusing and half-sad. Although making use of realistic elements only, Gogol is concerned not so much about objective descriptions, or the so-called local colour, as about that subjective vision of reality which he himself needs in order to have a rest from himself for a while. He may alter and exaggerate many details for such a purpose ; he may mix various seasons, or indulge in private comments of his own ; yet artistically he remains convincing throughout. Moreover, in reading the story we are soon overcome by a curious nostalgia—by that melancholy which arises in places of beautiful but vanished memories. It is the distant flapping of the wings of Time, as it were, which often transforms the story into a disguised elegy. Elegy and humour are mixed in it in such a way that we hardly know where one of them ends and the other begins : Gogol makes them inseparable. The story shows also a greater simplicity and a much slower tempo than the *Evenings*. True, he often deviates from the main theme, is too fond of *Kleinmalerei ;* yet he never tires us, but through the very accumulation of everyday trifles he keeps our interest growing until the very death of the owners, and the arrival of their " practical " heir who immediately adopts all modern innovations, with the result that he soon ruins himself, the estate, and the peasants.

If we now turn to *Taras Bulba*, which appeared in the same volume, we discover in it Gogol's finest romance pure and simple. Here he plunged once again into the old traditions of his homeland and brought back precious booty : a masterpiece saturated with the fragrance of the soil and with the Cossack past in all its picturesque though cruel grandeur. Although externally modelled on the romances of Walter Scott, *Taras Bulba* often reads more like a gorgeous folk-ballad. Besides, Gogol himself called it an epic. Its content is thrilling from the first to the last line, and its language is so melodious, so rhythmic, that it can intoxicate by its sheer music.

III

Taras Bulba has often been called the Cossack Iliad. It gives us in fact a broad picture of primitive Cossack life, a picture which is true, not historically, but poetically. The characters we see in it are whole and simple as those of the Iliad. Their inner world with its pre-moral " beyond good and evil " is almost the same as in the Greek epic ; and their passions too are equally impulsive and elemental. This can be said in particular of Gogol's central hero, the old Taras himself, who would make a magnificent figure in any folk-ballad or heroic epic.

We meet him first when he welcomes his two sons, Ostap and Andriy, on their return from the *bursa* (a kind of clerical college in old Kiev) and cunningly entices Ostap into a fight with him in order to see whether the young bursar would make a good Cossack. Pleased with the result of the fight, he decides at once to take his two sons to the distant Syetch—the Cossack headquarters of those days. The blood of an old warrior has awakened in him ; he is so impatient to witness the first exploits of his handsome lads that he wants to depart the very next morning. His withered and devoted wife cannot believe it. She hopes her sons will stop for a few days at home—she has not seen them for so many years, and her heart is overflowing with love, admiration, tenderness, pride and fear. But she knows her old Taras too well. Her last solace is to crouch all night on the ground, silently watching her two sons whom she may perhaps never see again. But the summer nights are short. She still has a faint hope that something might perhaps cause Taras to postpone the departure. The dawn dispels her last illusions : the Cossacks are bent on leaving their home. In despair she clings to the saddle of her favourite, Andriy ; she implores and cries and swoons—all is in vain. The two lads are bravely trying to hide their grief, while the stern Taras hardly bestows a glance upon the meek companion of his life : his thoughts are elsewhere. Soon we see him riding with his sons and a small retinue across the endless steppe.

"The farther they penetrated into the steppe, the more beautiful it became. Then all the south, even as far as the Black Sea, was a green, virgin wilderness. No plough had ever passed over the immeasurable waves of wild growth; horses alone, hidden in it as in a forest, trod it down. The whole surface resembled a golden-green ocean upon which were sprinkled millions of different flowers. Through the tall, slender stems of the grass peeped light-blue, dark-blue and lilac star-thistles; the yellow broom thrust up its pyramidal head; the parasol-shaped white flower of the false flax shimmered on high. A wheat-ear, brought God knows whence, was filling out to ripening. Amongst the roots of this luxuriant vegetation ran partridges with outstretched necks. The air was filled with the notes of a thousand different birds. On high hovered the hawks, with wings outspread, and their eyes fixed intently on the grass. The cries of a flock of wild ducks, ascending from one side, were echoed from God knows what distant lake. From the grass arose, with measured sweep, a gull, and skimmed wantonly through blue waves of air. And now she has vanished on high, and appears only as a black dot; now she has turned her wings and shines in the sun-light. Oh, steppes, how beautiful you are!

"Our travellers halted only a few minutes

for dinner and continued their journey until evening. In the evening the whole steppe changed its aspect. All its varied expanse was bathed in the last bright glow of the sun ; and as it grew dark it could be seen how the shadow flitted across it and it became dark green. The mist rose more densely ; each flower, each blade of grass, emitted a fragrance as of ambergris, and the whole steppe distilled perfume. Broad bands of rosy gold were streaked across the dark blue heaven, as with a gigantic brush ; here and there gleamed, in white tufts, light and transparent clouds : and the freshest, most enchanting of gentle breezes barely stirred the tops of the grass-blades, like sea-waves, and caressed the cheek. The music which had resounded through the day had died away, and given place to another. Striped marmots crept out of their holes, stood erect on their hind legs, and filled the steppe with their whistle. The whir of the grasshopper had become more distinctly audible. Sometimes the cry of the swan was heard from some distant lake, ringing through the air like a silver trumpet . . . Having supped, the Cossacks lay down to sleep, after hobbling their horses, and turning them out to graze. They lay down in their gabardines. The stars of night gazed upon them. They could hear the countless myriads of insects which filled the grass ; their rasping, whistling and chirping, softened by the fresh air, resounded clearly through the night, and lulled the drowsy ear. If one of them rose and stood for a time the steppe presented itself to him strewn with the sparks of glow-worms. At times the night sky was illumined in spots by the glare of burning reeds along pools or river bank ; and dark flights of swans flying to the north were suddenly lit up by the silvery, rose-coloured gleam, till it seemed as though red kerchiefs were floating in the heavens."*

With the same never-flagging verve, Gogol describes the arrival of Taras and his sons in Syetch : the boisterous life in the headquarters ; the child-like, irresponsible Cossack types ; the ruse with which the old Taras advocates an immediate expedition simply in order to give his sons a chance ; the drunken revel ; the election of a new Koshevoy ; the cruel, and in its very cruelty, tragi-comic pogrom ; the figure of the crafty Jew—Yankel ; the whole Cossack army on the move . . . Then he makes us witness the siege of Dubno during which Andriy learns that the beautiful Polish maiden, who had captivated his heart while he was still in Kiev, happens to be in the beleaguered and starving city. Listening to the voice of his love only, he goes

* All quotations are taken from the final version of *Taras Bulba* (1839-40). Its English translation appears in Everyman's Library.

over to the Poles ; and we follow him into the town itself—to see the ghastly pictures of starvation, his meeting with the beauty, the arrival of the Polish reinforcements, new engagements with the Cossacks, the capture of Ostap by the enemy, and at last the sortie of Polish horsemen headed by the renegade Andriy who is suddenly recognized, enticed into the wood and shot by the indignant Taras himself.

The Cossacks are beaten, dispersed. The old Taras is severely wounded. Weeks pass before he recovers, only to hear that his Ostap is imprisoned in Warsaw—awaiting, together with some other captured Cossacks, public torture and execution. But Taras knows his duty. With the help of Yankel he penetrates into Warsaw, and bribes the prison guard, but his plan is frustrated at the last moment. He is present, in disguise, at the gruesome execution of his own son. Then he leaves Warsaw. Soon, however, he reappears on the Polish border—with an army of a hundred and twenty thousand Cossacks whose *hetman* he has become. And he does not tarry with his vengeance. Raging like an elemental force let loose, he plunders and destroys entire districts. Remembering the death of Ostap, he is without mercy. He knows only one language—that of fire and sword. At last he is himself captured by the enemy, tied to a tree on the banks of the Dnyester, and set on fire. But even here he remains undaunted. When already licked by the flames he turns his eyes towards the river and beholds with satisfaction that his comrades are in the skiffs, rowing away, and beyond the reach of the Polish shots.

"Broad is the river Dnyester," so ends the epic, "and in it are many deep pools, dense reed-beds, clear shallows and little bays : its watery mirror gleams, filled with the melodious plaints of the swan, the proud wild goose glides swiftly over it ; and snipe, red-throated ruffs, and other birds are to be found among the reeds and along the banks. The Cossacks rowed swiftly on in the narrow double-ruddered boats—rowed stoutly, carefully shunning the sand-bars, and cleaving the ranks of the birds, which took wing—they rowed, and talked of their *hetman*."

Such is a bald outline of Gogol's great romance, which has but one drawback : the melodramatic love between Andriy and the Polish maiden. Quite apart from its being an old and conventional motive (the beloved in the camp of the enemy), it is bound to become somewhat pale in Gogol's hands for the simple reason that Gogol is not good at describing young women, or the love-scenes. In all his works we hardly find any love-scenes proper. The only exceptions are *Taras Bulba* and the *May Night* ; and even here women are painted with almost oleographic superlatives : " He raised his eyes and saw a beauty such as he had never beheld in all his life, black-eyed and with skin white as snow illumined by the dawning flush of the sun."

So far as is known, Gogol had no first-hand experience of a woman's love. There are even several indications that in matters of sex he had remained in an almost infantile stage. Without enumerating various " psycho-analytical " proofs from his writings or private letters, it can be said in spite of the patronizing tone with which he treated his mother after his father's death, that he never got rid of his infantile attachment to her. The consequence was that he was unable to project his love upon any other woman.* As his strong " mother-complex " never allowed him to approach a woman sexually, his notions of love were very abstract and platonic. At the same time his sexual craving as such tried to find independent satisfaction in auto-erotic practices, which ruined his nerves and were perhaps largely responsible for his moral self-disgust, his secretiveness, his continuous dread of God (the *all-seeing* Judge), and his equal dread of woman the temptress : woman as the symbol of

* When he had later fallen in love with Mme. Rosset-Smirnova, his love was entirely platonic, more like the love of a son for his mother than anything else.

the disgusting and yet diabolical power of the sex. Hence the curious fact that in his works he either idealizes women into ethereal unearthly beings, or sees in them demoniac agencies of hell and perdition.

One of his early fragments (published in 1830) is called *The Woman.* As it may throw a certain light upon Gogol's attitude towards *das ewig Weibliche*, it will be useful to quote at least these few passages : " We ripen and arrive at perfection, but when ? After we have more deeply and more completely comprehended woman ! What is woman ? The language of the gods. She is poetry, she is thought, and we are merely her reflection in reality. Her impressions shine upon us, and the more strongly, the more intensely they are reflected in ourselves, the nobler and better we become . . . Rob the world of its sunrays, and the bright variety of colours will disappear : heaven and earth will be confounded in a gloom darker even than the shores of the Styx. What is love ? One's spiritual home : man's beautiful craving for that past in which lies the immaculate origin of his existence : where there remains on everything the mysterious, imperishable trace of innocent childhood ; where everything is homeland. And whenever man's soul dissolves in the ethereal bosom of a woman's soul, when it finds in her its own father, the

Eternal God, its own brothers, feelings and phenomena which nothing on earth could express before, what happens to it then? Then the soul revives within itself its forgotten harmonies, its forgotten heavenly existence in the bosom of God Himself, and makes it infinity."

Lines such as these are of great psychological interest. Gogol's innate worship of the abstract Woman as the great eternal Mother made him sexually even more timid; for an excessive but one-sided idealism in this respect often makes one regard even the remotest sexual desire for a concrete woman as a kind of sacrilege. But while wanting to find himself in and through Woman, Gogol was at the same time afraid of real women. It is significant that his descriptions of *seductive* women are often as vivid as if he had been possessed now and then by burning erotic fancies, combined with an equally burning fear which he tried to combat at times by a kind of bantering and spiteful tone when talking of the other sex. The demoniac woman as he conceived her is particularly well symbolized in his *Viy*.

IV

This tale of the stoical "bursar" Homa who perishes through a witch of enthralling beauty, or rather, through the hellish agencies that are at her service, is the last work Gogol wrote in the same way as he did his *Evenings*, that is, by taking the subject straight from folk-lore. He himself acknowledges in a note that "*Viy* is a colossal product of folk-imagination. The Little Russians call so the chief of the gnomes, whose eyelids are so long that they touch the ground. The whole story is a popular tradition. I did not want to alter it in any way, and I relate it in the same manner as I heard it myself."

Without investigating how far Gogol's remark about alterations corresponds to truth, we can say that this story too reads like an intensified folk-tale, in which whimsical realistic touches (the descriptions of the bursars or of the Cossacks) are mixed with the wildest romantic fancies and visions. At the same time we can notice that whenever Gogol takes up folk-loristic motives, he unconsciously chooses those only through which he can veil or discharge his own "complexes". The most typical personal modifications of such motives are represented by the *Cruel Vengeance* (the incest-motive) in the *Evenings*, and by the *Viy* (the dreaded ancestor-imago, etc.) in *Mirgorod*. Apart from this, he often envelops his "symbols" in most incredible and grotesque settings. So much so that *Viy* could easily rival the weirdest fantasies by an Edgar Allan Poe. Take, for example, its finale.

The intrepid philosopher, Homa, was shut for the third time in the church, where he had to read all the night prayers besides the corpse of the beautiful witch, for whose death he was partly responsible. In order to overcome his fear he had drunk a fair amount of brandy, and now he was turning page after page by the flickering candles which threw a yellow light upon the coffin. " Suddenly—in the dead silence —the iron lid of the coffin burst open with a crash and up rose the corpse. She was even more terrifying than before. Her teeth grated together horribly, her lips twitched in convulsions, and the air was filled with wild, whining invocations. A whirlwind rose about the church, the holy ikons fell to the ground and the shattered glass of the little windows came showering down from above. The doors were torn from their hinges and a countless host of monsters flew into the church, filling the whole building with a fearful noise of flapping wings and scratching claws as they circled about searching everywhere for the philosopher. The last fumes of drunkenness left Homa's head. He just kept on crossing himself and reading prayers, no matter what took place. All the time he could hear the obscene host dashing around him, almost scraping him with the tips of their wings and hideous tails. He had not sufficient courage to examine them ; yet he could discern the form of some enormous monster covering the whole of one wall : it was enveloped in its own tangled hair, as in a wood, and through the net of hair two eyes with slightly raised brows peered out in a horrid fashion. Above him something like a huge bubble hung in the air, with a thousand claws and stings protruding from its middle. Black earth clung to them in clots. All were looking at Homa, seeking him, but unable to see him, surrounded as he was by his magic circle.

" ' Bring the Viy ! ' rang out the voice of the corpse, ' go and bring the Viy in ! ' And suddenly all became silent in the church. A kind of wolfish howling was heard in the distance, and soon the church resounded with heavy footsteps. Casting a glance downwards, Homa saw them leading forward some burly, thickset, bow-legged figure, covered with black soil : his earthy arms and legs stuck out like powerful sinewy roots. He walked heavily along, stumbling at every step. His eyelids hung down to the very ground. Homa noticed in terror that his face was of iron. They led him by the arms straight to the place where Homa stood.

" ' Lift my eyelids ! I cannot see ! " said

the Viy in a subterranean tone, and all the throng dashed forward to raise them for him.

" 'Don't look!' some inner voice whispered to the philosopher. But he could not refrain, and looked.

" 'There he is!" shouted the Viy, and pointed with his iron finger at him. The whole crowd flung themselves upon the philospher. Lifeless he crashed down on the floor: his soul flew out of his body from sheer terror. Here a cock-crow was heard. It was the second crowing, for the gnomes had missed the first. In their dismay they dashed now headlong at the doors and windows in order to get out as quickly as possible; but it was too late. And so they all remained there stuck fast in the doors and windows of the church. The priest who came in the morning stopped aghast at the sight of such desecration of God's sanctuary, and dared not give in it the burial service. So the church remained ever after with the monsters stuck in their places. It became overgrown with shrubs and trees, with roots and wild thorns, and no one could now find his way to it."

However involved such purely fantastic motives may be, they usually have a certain relation not only to Ukrainian folk-lore, but also to Gogol himself. His exaggerated introspection made him keenly aware of his own defects—a feature which led him to continuous moral dissatifsaction and hypochondria on the one hand, and to continuous reserve on the other. So it happened that he suffered from a double urge : to mask and mystify everything about himself, and at the same to confess, or even to whip publicly all his inner " nastiness ". These two contradictory propensities may throw some light upon Gogol's instinctive choice of themes and symbols, upon his style, and also upon his grotesque humour, by means of which he said indirectly many things he would never mention in a straightforward way. The gruesome Viy, for instance, with clots of earth clinging to him and with eyes which bring death when they *see*, expresses certain subconscious fears and terrors of Gogol himself—terrors and fears connected with his abnormal erotic habits. And his vision of the monsters that remained stuck fast in the doors and windows of God's sanctuary is perhaps not quite casual either : Gogol's life was a long and painful effort to free his own soul from those monsters of imperfection which remained stuck in it and haunted his morbid imagination with all the horrors of eternal doom. Anyhow, even if we abstain, for the time being, from going deeper into this matter, we may safely repeat that most themes used and elaborated by Gogol, whether they be fantastic or " realistic ", have some relation or other to his own intimate self. In this respect he is perhaps the most *personal* of all Russian authors. His art depended very largely on his own " complexes " which can be traced even in such an innocent and apparently objective story as the *Quarrel between Ivan Ivanovitch and Ivan Nikiforovitch.* However, it is always useful to remember that even when such " complexes " determine (subconsciously) the choice of motive and symbols of a work of art, its esthetic value nevertheless depends only on the amount of real talent. And Gogol's grotesque quarrel of the two Ivans certainly shows great talent in every line.

The story itself is again a simple anecdote deepened and enlarged into something more significant. Gogol, who took his material where he found it, was probably influenced by Naryezhny's *The Two Ivans, or Passion for Litigation* (1825) ; yet the treatment and the thematic development of the story could have been done only by such a master of the grotesque as Gogol himself.

To begin with, two worthies of Mirgorod are introduced to us. " Ivan Ivanovitch is tall and thin ; Ivan Nikiforovitch is rather shorter in stature but makes it up in thickness. Ivan Ivanovitch's head is like a radish, tail down ; Ivan Nikiforovitch's like a radish with the tail up. Ivan Ivanovitch lolls on the balcony in his shirt sleeves after dinner only ; in the evening he dons his pelisse and goes out somewhere, either to the village shop, where he supplies flour, or into the field to catch quail. Ivan Nikiforovitch lies all day at his porch : if the days are not too hot he generally turns his back to the sun and will not go anywhere. Ivan Ivanovitch is a very refined man, never utters an impolite word in conversation, and is offended at once if he hears one. Ivan Nikiforovitch is not always on his guard. On such occasions, Ivan Ivanovitch usually rises from his seat and says, 'Enough, enough, Ivan Nikiforovitch ! It's better to go out at once than to utter such godless words.' Ivan Nikiforovitch is fond of bathing : and when he is up to the neck in water, orders a table and a samovar, or tea urn, to be placed on the water, for he is very fond of drinking tea in that cool position. Ivan Ivanovitch has large, expressive eyes of a snuff-colour, and a mouth shaped something like the letter V ; Ivan Nikiforovitch has small, yellowish eyes, quite concealed between heavy brows and fat cheeks ; and his nose is the shape of a ripe plum. If Ivan Ivanovitch treats you to snuff, he always licks the cover of his box first with his tongue, then taps on it with his finger and says as he raises it, if you are an acquaintance, 'Dare I beg you, sir, to give me the pleasure ?' if a stranger, 'Dare I beg you, sir, though I have not the honour of knowing your rank, name and family, to do me the favour ?' but Ivan Nikiforovitch puts his box straight into your hand and merely adds, 'Do me the favour.' Neither Ivan Ivanovitch nor Ivan Nikiforovitch will, on any account, admit a Jew with his wares without purchasing of him remedies against insects, after having first rated him well for belonging to the Hebrew faith. But in spite of numerous dissimilarities, Ivan Ivanovitch and Ivan Nikiforovitch are both very fine fellows."

These two Ivans are in short two antitheses and yet inseparable friends, as inseparable as if they were one human being, as if "the devil himself had bound them together with a rope" ; where one goes the other follows. Yet nothing is constant in this world, not even the friendship of such model citizens as the two Ivans from Mirgorod. Their friendship came in fact to a premature end through a sheer trifle. This is how it happened : Ivan Nikiforovitch had a gun, just an ordinary old gun which was of no use to him at all. Ivan Ivanovitch saw the gun one morning and wanted to buy it. He broached the subject very diplomatically, but his gruff friend did not wish to part with his useless weapon even when Ivan Ivanovitch offered for it a sow and two sacks of oats. Diplomatic pourparlers soon passed into arguments.

" ' Excuse me, Ivan Ivanovitch, my gun is a choice thing, a most curious thing ; and besides, it is a very agreeable decoration in a room.'

" ' You go on like a fool about that gun of yours, Ivan Nikiforovitch,' said Ivan Ivanovitch, with vexation ; for he was beginning to be really angry.

" ' And you, Ivan Ivanovitch, are a regular goose ! '

" If Ivan Nikiforovitch had not uttered that word they would not have quarrelled, but would have parted friends as usual ; but now things took quite another turn. Ivan Ivanovitch flew into a rage.

" ' What was it you said, Ivan Nikiforovitch ? ' he said, raising his voice.

" ' I said you were like a goose, Ivan Ivanovitch ! '

" ' How dare you, sir, forgetful of decency and the respect due to a man's rank and family, insult him with such a disgraceful name ! '

" ' What is there disgraceful about it ? And why are you flourishing your hands so, Ivan Ivanovitch ? '

" ' How dared you, I repeat, in disregard of all decency, call me a goose ? "

" ' I spit on your head, Ivan Ivanovitch ! What are you screeching about ? '

" Ivan Ivanovitch could no longer control himself. His lips quivered ; his mouth lost its usual V shape and became like the letter O ; he glared so that he was terrible to look at."

In a word, their friendship passed into hatred. To the great surprise of the whole town they not only became mortal enemies, but soon found themselves in the law-court, accusing each other of all possible offences and crimes, of planned murders, of high treason, and even of atheism.

The litigation went on and on. But one day a solemn and important event took place. The local chief of police gave a reception. " Whence shall I obtain the brush and colours to depict this varied gathering and magnificent feast? Take your watch, open it and look what is going on inside. A fearful confusion, is it not? Now, imagine almost the same, if not a greater number of wheels standing in the chief of police's courtyard. How many carriages and waggons were there! One was wide behind and narrow in front, another narrow behind and wide in front. One was a carriage and waggon combined ; another neither a carriage nor a waggon. One resembled a huge hay-rick or a fat merchant's wife ; another a dilapidated Jew or a skeleton not quite freed from the skin. One was a perfect pipe with long stem in profile ; another resembling nothing whatever, suggested some strange, fantastic object. In the midst of this chaos of wheels rose coaches with windows like those of a room. The drivers in grey Cossack coats, gabardines, and white hareskin coats, sheepskin hats and caps of various patterns, and with pipes in their hands, drove the unharnessed horses through the yard."

Now, by a ruse, the chief of police had managed to bring the two Ivans together. They sat at his house at the same table, silently helping to swallow the interminable number of dishes, and without looking at each other. When the dinner was over they both rose from their seats with the obvious intention of running away. But here the sly host beckoned. And "Ivan Ivanovitch—not our Ivan Ivanovitch, but the other with one eye—got behind Ivan Nikiforovitch and the chief stepped behind Ivan Ivanovitch, and the two began to drag them backwards, in order to bring them together, and not release them till they had shaken hands with each other. . . . In spite of the fact that the friends resisted to the best of their ability, they were nevertheless brought together, for the two chief movers received reinforcements from the ranks of their guests.

"'God be with you, Ivan Nikiforovitch and Ivan Ivanovitch! Declare upon your honour now, that what you quarrelled about were mere trifles, were they not? Are you not ashamed of yourselves before people and before God ? '

" ' I do not know,' said Ivan Nikiforovitch, panting with fatigue, though it is to be observed that he was not at all disinclined to a reconciliation. ' I do not know what I did to Ivan Ivanovitch, but why did he destroy my coop and plot against my life ? '

" ' I am innocent of any evil designs,' said Ivan Ivanovitch, never looking at Ivan Nikiforovitch. ' I swear before God and before you, honourable noblemen, I did nothing to my enemy. Why does he calumniate me and insult my rank and family ? '

" ' How have I insulted you, Ivan Ivanovitch ? ' said Ivan Nikiforovitch. One moment more of explanation and the long enmity would have been extinguished. Ivan Nikiforovitch was already feeling in his pocket for his snuffbox, and was about to say, ' Do me the favour ? '

" ' Is it not an insult,' answered Ivan Ivanovitch, without raising his eyes, ' when you, my dear sir, insulted my honour and my family with a word which it is improper to repeat here ? '

" ' Permit me to observe in a friendly manner, Ivan Ivanovitch '—here Ivan Nikiforovitch touched Ivan Ivanovitch's button with his finger, which clearly indicated the disposition of his mind—' that you took offence, the deuce only knows at what, because I called you a *goose*—'

" It occurred to Ivan Nikiforovitch that he had made a mistake in uttering that word ; but it was too late ; the word was said. Everything went to the winds. . . ."

His opponent " gave one look at Ivan Nikiforovitch, but such a look ! If that look had possessed active power, then it would have turned Ivan Nikiforovitch into dust. The guests understood the look and hastened to separate them. And this man, the very model of gentleness rushed out in a fearful rage. Such violent storms do passions produce ! "

The old quarrel between the two Ivans became now even more intense. They both resumed their former law-suits and dragged them on for years and years. Much time had elapsed before Gogol happened to pass through Mirgorod and see once more the two enemies. They were both grey-haired and dilapidated, but they were still wasting all their time and their last money in the Courts of Justice, hoping to ruin each other. And the whole place looked so grey and dismal.

While the first quarrel is described by Gogol in a comic vein, this second quarrel after the unsuccessful attempt at a reconciliation, has a decidedly tragic aspect. Gogol achieves this change simply by a transposition of his own standpoint : up to the second climax (when the word "goose" spoils the chance of reconciliation) Gogol uses such a tone as if he himself were on the same level as both Ivans ; after it, however, he deliberately takes his stand above them, as well as above Mirgorod, looking upon all *sub specie* of life in general. And the melancholy note of the finale is all the stronger because of the comic contrast in the previous chapters of the story.

"The lean nags known in Mirgorod as post-horses began to stamp their hoofs, which were buried in a grey mass of mud, with a sound very displeasing to the ear. The rain poured in torrents upon the Jew seated on the box, covered with a rug. The dampness penetrated me through and through. The gloomy barrier with a sentry-box in which an old soldier was repairing his weapons, was passed slowly. Again the same fields, in some places black where they had been dug up, in others of a greenish hue ; wet daws and crows ; monotonous rain ; a tearful sky, without one gleam of light ! . . . It is gloomy in this world, gentlemen !"

V

Thus the story of the two Ivans is again a blending of comedy and tragedy. Another feature which one begins to feel in this piece very strongly is the fact that Gogol moulds his figures with the temperament and the perception of an actor. Hence his vivacity, his *sans gêne* with the reader, his inimitable dialogue, his keen sense for all that is grotesque in man. Wishing to assert himself against people, against life, against reality as a whole, he does so by means of his laughter and sarcasms which he employs preferably in the manner of a malicious impersonator. Therefore he has a sharp eye for all that is ridiculous in man's physical appearance and in his everyday habits. Gogol never shows us a man's soul or spirit in the way Dostoevsky does. When he wants to give us an indication of the inner selves of his heroes he suggests it as a rule only through their physique, especially through the grotesque and the absurd side of their physique, or through some equally absurd ways of their daily lives.

This is an example of his portraiture (taken from the story of the two Ivans): " Agafya wore a cap on her head and a coffee-coloured cloak with yellow flowers, and had three warts on her nose. Her figure was like a cask, and it would be as hard to tell where to look for her waist as for her to see her nose without a mirror. Her feet were small and shaped like two cushions. She talked scandal, ate boiled beet-soup in the morning, and swore desperately ; and amongst all these various occupations her countenance never for an instant changed its expression, which phenomenon, as a rule, women alone are capable of displaying."

And most of Gogol's works abound in similar characteristics. They are usually a clever summing up of trifles, of grotesque details and comparisons, such as this : " It must be said that the officials of the Palace of Justice were distinguished by their ugliness and unprepossessing appearance. Some had faces like badly baked bread, with a cheek swollen out on one side, and the chin bent in the other direction, with a pimple on the upper lip, which was cracked, moreover—in fact they were anything but pretty. They all spoke gruffly in a voice that sounded as if they were just going to hit someone." Or take another of his descriptions : " The landlord of the little house in which Tchertkov lodged belonged to the class of persons who are numerous in Russia and whose character is as difficult to describe as the colour of a threadbare overcoat. In his youth he had been a captain in the army, a loud-voiced bully, and had also been engaged in civilian pursuits, was a capital hand at administering a sound thrashing, and was at the same time a sharp fellow, a dandy and a fool, but in his old age he blended all these striking peculiarities into a sort of dingy indefiniteness. He was a widower, was on the shelf, was no longer spruce, neither bragged nor quarrelled, was fond of his cup of tea, and of babbling all sorts of nonsense over it ; he walked about his room snuffing his candle ends : punctually every month called on his lodgers for the rent ; went out into the street with the key in his hand to have a look at the roof of his house ; continually routed out the porter from the cupboard in which the latter used to secrete himself for a nap ; in short, he was on the shelf, a man who from all the ups and downs of his turbulent existence had retained nothing but vulgar habits."

Gogol depicts people always from the outside : from what is visible to the eye and particularly from what can be impersonated. Having first *collected* as many trifles as possible, he arranges them in a mosaic-like way until the person stands before us alive, but alive with a kind of static, almost frozen intensity, which makes sometimes even the most ordinary people look rather like ghosts. Gogol never tires of collecting various data, but immediately his imagination gets hold of some fact or other it is always inclined to exaggerate it—" to develop it in the shape of most terrible apparitions which torture me so much that I cannot sleep and am losing all my strength." The only thing that saved him from being too often tortured by his own imagination in this way was his humour. It saved him from several other things as well. For as long as he was able to ridicule the unpleasant and offensive aspects of life, turning them into the grotesque, he could always gain relief, partly at least, from their bad psychic effects. Laughter thus became the best medicine against his own over-developed and *intensifying* imagination, which threatened to undermine him inwardly. So much so that when, later on, Gogol became only serious and solemn, morally solemn, his creative output decreased, and he finally collapsed under the weight of his own " inner disorganization ".

Chapter Four

GOGOL'S PETERSBURG STORIES

I

THE dominant mood of Gogol's *Evenings* and *Mirgorod* is that of the south. All their subjects, without exception, are connected with the Ukraine. Southern sun and temper simmer on so many of their pages that one would hardly believe they had been written in Petersburg where " everything is wet, flat, pale, grey, foggy." However, in this grey and foggy city Gogol soon found new materials for his further works. Owing to the fact that he felt a complete alien in its artificial atmosphere, he was all the more aware of its unpleasant, its loathsome features. And he began to " collect " them in the same way as he had formerly collected his Ukraininan motives, reminiscences and impressions.

Feeling more and more uprooted in this life, he now tried to assert himself against it by showing its vulgarity, its unworthiness. This new period developed in him almost simulatneously with his *Mirgorod*, and it soon found an expression in his Petersburg stories—*The Nevsky Prospect*, *A Madman's Diary*, *The Portrait*, *The Nose*, and the famous *Cloak*.* The first three of these stories were published in his *Arabesques* (1835)—a motley collection of essays on history, art, architecture, poetry, and even on geography. The whole book is interesting chiefly as a proof that Gogol had not yet entirely found himself and was still groping after his real vocation, wavering as it were between a writer, a " savant ", and also a preacher and educator. Yet whenever he abandoned his proper sphere—that of a story writer—he became both commonplace and pretentious. Even his views on art, as expounded in the *Arabesques*, are not at all original ; they show a strong influence of that romantic-esthetic school which had adopted the principles of the Germans, Schelling and Wackenroder.** Gogol's articles may sometimes surprise one by acute observations, yet they hardly abound in new thoughts. Apart from this, he talks with great *aplomb* of things he does not know much about, trying to conceal his lack of competence in a language which is too rhetorical to be above suspicion. " If essays of

* *The Overcoat*, in Mrs. Garnett's translation.

** Both of them had adherents in Russia, particularly in Moscow, such as Odoevsky, Shevyryov, etc.

this kind are called scientific, then may God preserve us from such science ", remarked Bielinsky after the perusal of the book. But he was enthusiastic about the three stories—*The Portrait*, *The Nevsky Prospect* and *A Madman's Diary*—which were printed in it, and he was right.* The stories are really good enough to redeem even a worse collection of essays than the *Arabesques*. Gogol still indulges, at times, in his habitual exuberance, even in melodramatic remarks and exclamations, but all such defects pass almost unnoticed in the general excellence of the whole.

II

The Portrait, which is by far the worst of the three stories, reminds us once more of that Gogol who had written *The Cruel Vengeance* and *Viy*. It deals with the demoniac element in life ; only this time Gogol leans not upon folk-lore, but upon Western romanticism. There is nothing specifically " Russian " in this story. It could

* In the *Arabesques* appeared three more narrative fragments of minor importance : an allegorical poem in prose called " Life," a " Chapter from a Historical Novel " (printed for the first time in 1831) and " The Prisoner " (written in 1830). The last two are fragments of a planned historical novel, *Hetman*, the first half of which is supposed to have been written and then burnt by Gogol.

easily have been written by a German, by any European author. It is even slightly reminiscent of Hoffmann's *Elixiere des Teufels*, of Maturin's *Melmoth* (which Gogol had probably read in a Russian translation), and also of some other romantic works.

Its theme is the tragedy of a young artist, Chertkov, who had been seduced by some satanic power to exchange his genius for worldly fame and success. This power was embodied in an old man's portrait, particularly in its eyes which looked as though something of life had been retained in them, something which filled one with the sensation of inexplicable horror. Chertkov found the portrait in an old shop, but just when he was on the point of buying it he became so frightened by it that he ran out of the shop. Yet when he came home he found the mysterious picture on the walls of his studio. How did it get there? Who could have brought it? He was unable to find any reasonable explanation of its re-appearance. However, the portrait was there, and its life-like eyes gazed terribly in the moonlight which they seemed to absorb. The canvas itself vanished as it were, and the old man stared out of the frame as though out of a window. He haunted Chertkov every minute, pursued him even in sleep with ominous nightmares and suggestions. And the advice he gave him in one of the nightmares was very simple : he wanted Chertkov to replace all his endless toil and striving after perfection in art by easy success. For " everything in the world is done for profit. Make haste and paint the portraits of all the town ! Accept every commission, but do not be in love with your work ; don't sit over it day and night : Time flies quickly, and life will not lag behind. The more pictures you finish in the day, the more money there will be in your pocket and the more glory you will win."

The next morning Chertkov's landlord came either to get the rent from him or to make him clear out of the studio. For greater safety he brought a policeman. Being without money, Chertkov began to argue. Here the policeman grasped the frame of the strange portrait somewhat too tightly, and out of the frame there fell a number of golden ducats rolling on the floor. The artist was now saved from all inconveniences. He felt the whole world belonged to him. He rented at once the finest studio he could find. After a few rich " sitters " with whose taste and demands he had complied, he made himself talked about in society, became the vogue, with the obvious result that he was flooded with commissions. Condescending to the public taste, Chertkov soon buried the last sparks of his talent in the bundles of bank-notes which were steadily increasing in his coffers. He was now a recognised *maestro* ; and the colder, the emptier his soul was growing the more self-satisfied he became, until one day—when he was at the very height of his worldly success—something unexpected happened : he was invited to pronounce his opinion of a picture sent in by a young painter who had sacrificed everything for the sake of his talent and lived only for his true vocation. Chertkov looked at the picture and remained numb : " Pure, stainless, lovely as a bride, the painter's work stood before him. And not the faintest sign of desire to dazzle, of pardonable vanity, even of any thought of showing off to the crowd could be seen in it . . . The features of these godlike faces seemed to be breathing with the mysteries which the soul has no power, no means to convey to another : the inexpressible found serene expression in them ; and all this was flung on to the canvas so lightly, with such modest freedom, that it might have seemed the fruit of a moment's inspiration dawning upon the artist's mind." And while looking at this true work of art, Chertkov suddenly realized what a terrible price he had paid for his own fame and success. He realized what he himself could have become had he not prostituted his own gift. He returned home with a firm decision to make up for the lost opportunity and he set to work at once.

Yet although he did his best to get rid of all those cheap mannerisms which had brought him fame and money, his brush would not obey him : his talent had died long since. In his impotence he soon fell a prey to such maddening envy that other people's talents made him rage with fury. He went so far as to start buying, even at the highest prices, those new pictures which bore the stamp of talent, and having brought them home, tore them into pieces with the delight of a lunatic. All the wealth he had amassed before he spent now in this manner. Fortunately, his envy soon developed into real madness which brought an end to his life.

Such is the first part of the story. Its second part is only a mechanical addition with the object of explaining the secret of the portrait itself. For we find the portrait once more, at an auction, and the son of the artist who had painted it relates its history. He transfers us into a dull suburb of Petersburg where once a mysterious money-lender, called Petromihali, lived. The strange thing about him was that his money invariably ruined whomever he had helped, for he was the embodiment of the Antichrist who wanted to perpetuate evil on earth. One day, however, the narrator's father was called to the usurer's house. Petromihali was on his death-bed, and asked the artist to paint his face. The artist, trying to be " true to nature " had just finished the eyes of the old usurer when suddenly he became so terrified by the evil influence emanating from them that he refused to go on with his work. The old man implored him, offered him money, and in order to move him to pity, he even revealed the reason of why he wanted to be painted : " After my death I must go to Him, to Whom I am loth to go ; there I must endure tortures of which you have never dreamed ; but I need not go to Him as long as our earth stands, if only you finish the portrait. I have learned that half my life will pass into my portrait, if only it is painted by a skilful artist. You see that part of my life has gone into the eyes already ; it will be in all the features when you have finished. And though my body will rot, half of life will remain on earth, and for long ages I shall escape from torment."

The artist ran away in horror, but he found the unfinished portrait of the usurer on the wall of his house. He tried to burn it, but even the flames could not destroy the work which now began to sow evil everywhere. At last, pursued by his own work, he went into a monastery, took the vows, and submitted meekly to the severest monastic rules. Having purified himself through many devout and ascetic practices, he felt ready to paint a holy picture, that of the

Mother of God, in the church belonging to the monastery. Only after this did the eyes of the money-lender cease to haunt him, and the portrait vanished no one knew how and where. Eventually he imparted the whole secret to his son who, after a long separation, came to see him : " Listen, my son. For long years the Antichrist has craved to be born . . . Even now he is being born already, but only some parts of him can force their way into the world. He is choosing man himself for his dwelling-place, and appearing in those people whose angel seems to have abandoned them at their very birth and who are branded with terrible hatred towards men and everything that is the work of the Creator. Such was that marvellous money-lender, whom I, accursed as I was, dared to depict with my sinful brush. It was he, my son, it was Antichrist . . . In those loathsome evil eyes the devilish feeling persisted. Marvel, my son, at the terrible power of the devil. He strives to make his way into everything ; into our deeds, into our thoughts, and even into the inspiration of the artist. Innumerable will be the victims of that hellish spirit that lives unseen without form on earth. It is that same black spirit which forces itself upon us even in moments of the purest and holiest meditation. Ah, if my brush had not abandoned its hellish work, he would have done us even more evil, and there is no human power to resist him, for he is choosing that time when the greatest calamities are coming upon us. Woe to poor humanity, my son ! But listen to what the Mother of God herself revealed to me in an hour of holy vision . . . I learned that, in reward for my toils and my prayers, the supernatural existence of that demon in the portrait would not be eternal, that, if someone shall solemnly tell its story when fifty years have passed, at the time of the new moon, its force will be extinguished and will be scattered like dust, and I learned that I might tell you this before my death."

As it happens, at the very time of the auction fifty years had elapsed ; when the narrator had finished his story the portrait of the money-lender suddenly began to vanish from the canvas ; in its stead there appeared an insignificant landscape. Thus finishes the first version of the portrait. Its second version, however, which was written a few years later* and made the first part of the story much stronger and inwardly convincing, has a more fatalistic ending. According to it, the narrator " did not finish his sentence, but turned his eyes to the wall in order to glance

* The first version has been translated into English by Mrs. Garnett (*The Works of Nikolay Gogol*, Vol. III, *Chatto & Windus*, and the second is to be found in *Taras Bulba and Other Stories*, (Everyman's Library.)

once more at the portrait. The entire throng of auditors made the same movement, seeking the wonderful portrait with their eyes. But to their extreme amazement, it was no longer on the wall. An indistinct murmur and exclamation ran through the crowd, and then was heard the word 'stolen'. Someone had succeeded in carry- it off, taking advantage of the fact that the attention of the spectators was distracted by the story. And those present remained long in a state of surprise, not knowing whether they had really seen those remarkable eyes, or whether it was simply a dream which had floated for an instant before their eyesight, strained with long gazing at old pictures."

III

I have had to dwell on this story longer than would seem necessary because of its autobiographical interest. Not only do we see in it Gogol's personal attitude towards the problem of the relation between art and life, but also his fixed idea that the world "lieth in evil". The devil whom Gogol sees in the world is a projection of his own feeling of sinfulness—magnified by his imagination, by his superstitious fear, by his vision of eternal punishment. Psychologically *The Portrait* is closely connected with Gogol's *Viy*. At the same time it indicates certain further complications of his own inner life.

That problem of the ethical value of art, which later on played such havoc with him, is here anticipated—symbolically, of course—almost in the same shape in which he himself had to face it a few years later. For he, too, became eventually haunted by the portraits created by his own pen ; and in many respects he reacted not unlike the artist who had painted the Antichrist, that is, through mortification, asceticism, and passionate endeavours to become *morally* worthy of depicting " positive " and holy subjects. However, as this side of Gogol's inner drama will be dealt with in one of the next chapters, we can return to the other two stories printed in *The Arabesques*. Both of them, *The Nevsky Prospect* and *A Madman's Diary* are interesting, above all, by the fact that they are written on a " realistic " plane, but with a romantic temper. Once more Gogol goes to reality in order to expose it, to vent upon it his offended idealism, to overwhelm it with his indictments and with his bitter laughter. And again he does not copy—he only pieces together out of the collected fragments of life a mosaic which though realistic in all its details is subjective as a whole. And with all this it is artistically true and convincing.

Take *The Nevsky Prospect*. Gogol begins with a magnificent description of the Nevsky Thoroughfare. We see its lively crowds, varying at every hour of the day, and almost every sentence is enlivened by a whimsical allusion or remark on the part of the author himself. At twelve o'clock, for example, " tutors of all nationalities make a descent upon the Nevsky Prospect with their young charges in fine cambric collars. English Joneses and French Kocks walk arm in arm with the nurslings entrusted to their parental care, and with becoming dignity explain to them that the signboards over the shops are put there that people may know what is to be found within. Governesses, pale misses, and rosy mademoiselles walk majestically behind their light and nimble charges, bidding them hold themselves more upright or not drop their left shoulder ; in short, at this hour the Nevsky Prospect plays its pedagogic part. But as two o'clock approaches, the governesses, tutors and children are fewer ; and finally are crowded out by their tender papas walking arm in arm with their gaudy, variegated and hysterical spouses. Gradually these are joined by all who have finished their rather important domestic duties, such as talking to the doctor about the weather and the pimple that has come out on their nose, enquiring after the health of their horses, and their promising and gifted children, reading in the newspapers a leading article and the announcements of the arrivals and departures, and finally drinking a cup of tea or coffee. . . ." In this way one group passes, a new one comes along, then a second, a third, until the liveliest time has arrived—the hour of dusk. But the Nevsky deceives at all hours and "most of all when night falls in masses of shadow on it, throwing into relief the white and dun-coloured walls of the houses, when all the town is transformed into noise and brilliance, when myriads of carriages roll over bridges, postillions shout and jolt up and down on their horses, and when the demon himself lights the street lamps to show everything in false colours."

It is on such an evening that two friends—an artist, and an officer—walk in the cròwd and suddenly stop ; both of them are struck by the beauty of two women who happen to pass by, one after the other. The young lieutenant Pirogov (a devil-may-care type) rushes at once after the unknown blonde, while his friend, the dreamy artist Piskaryov, timidly follows the other woman who seems lovely and perfect as the Bianca of Perugino. He walks behind her in silent adoration, full of that instantaneous love which overpowers one like a kind of sweet madness. But at the end of his romantic errand he discovers that she lives in a house of ill-fame.

Offended by this divergence between reality and dream, outraged in all his purest instincts, he soon takes to drugs which alone are still capable of putting a veil over the vulgar truth of life. His sensitive nature is too weak to bear his own disgust, and he commits suicide.

As a grotesque counterpart to this drama, Pirogov's exploits are described. The blonde he pursues happens to be the rather pretty, rather stupid and also somewhat easy-going wife of a German artisan. Pirogov bravely follows her right into her house, calls again, and flirts with her under the very nose of her husband, Schiller—a regular German, who already at the age of twenty had mapped out his whole life, decided to save a capital of 50,000 roubles in the course of ten years and arranged all his affairs accordingly. He always got up punctually at seven, dined punctually at two, kissed his legal spouse only twice in the twenty-four hours, and got drunk only on Sundays.

This worthy and most respectable German husband suddenly caught Pirogov showering kisses upon his precious better half, showering them on her without any ceremony whatever. As this happened to be on a Sunday, the consternation of Schiller was aggravated by the already consumed beer. So he, too, forgot all about ceremonies and mercilessly thrashed the unwanted guest—in which undertaking he was gladly joined by his two equally drunken associates, the comrade Kuntz and the comrade Hoffmann. Besides himself with anger, the smart Pirogov set out at once to lodge a complaint with the general. His intention was to demand an exemplary punishment for the offenders. However, " all this ended rather strangely ; on the way he went into a café, ate two jam puffs, read something out of *The Northern Bee* and left the café with his wrath somewhat cooled. Then a pleasant fresh evening led him to take a few turns along the Nevsky, by nine o'clock he had recovered his serenity and decided that he had better not disturb the general on Sunday. And so he went to spend the evening with one of the directors of the control committee, where he met a very agreeable party of government officials and officers of his regiment. There he spent a very pleasant evening, and so distinguished himself in the mazurka that not only the ladies, but even their partners were moved to admiration."

The same mixture of profound tragedy and almost farcical comedy we find in *A Madman's Diary*. The underlying theme of this study is again the eternal divergence between reality and dream. Poprischin, an elderly copyist with a wrinkled face, clumsy manners and tufts of hair resembling hay, secretly falls in love with his chief's daughter. He has not the remotest chance of being even noticed by her ; there are too many Kammerjunkers and generals who snatch away everything that is really worth while. But Poprischin's humiliated and suppressed ego finds a compensation in dreams. The world of fancy gradually gets hold of him, and the harder the blows of life, the more exalted become those shelters in which he takes refuge. When at last the wedding of His Excellency's daughter (to a brilliant Kammerjunker of course) is announced, Poprischin's reason gives way. Having read in the papers that the Spanish throne is vacant, he ponders with great concern about the political affairs of that country and at last imagines he himself is Ferdinand VII, the king of Spain, in hiding. His demeanour changes accordingly. He patiently awaits the deputation of the " Spanish grandees " who appear eventually in order to take him to the lunatic asylum. But once in the asylum he interprets everything in harmony with his own fixed idea. During the painful cure-procedure he has a flash of the terrible truth. A piercing shriek of despair and an impulse to fly away from the world on a troika as quick as the wind, escape his breast. Then madness closes upon him again. His despair is replaced by the idiotic exclamation : " And do you know that the Bey of Algiers has a boil just under his nose ? "

The gradual transition of Poprischin's muddled state of mind into complete insanity is shown with such intuition as if Gogol himself had actually passed through the whole of it. On the surface the madman's fancies appear to be without head or tail ; yet there is a great deal of subconscious logic in their nonsensical " symbolism ". A psycho-analyst could easily discover in this work many clues to Gogol's own suppressed impulses. The important fact, however, is that *A Madman's Diary* is not only a reliable pathological document, but above all a perfect work of art. And its general tone is again that of a grotesque tragedy, in which Gogol always excels. Take as an example this entry, dated—*Madrid, February thirtieth :*

" And so here I am in Spain, and it happened so quickly that I can hardly realize it yet. This morning the Spanish deputies arrived and I got into a carriage with them. The extraordinary rapidity of our journey struck me as strange. We went at such a rate that within half an hour we had reached the frontiers of Spain. But of course now there are railroads all over Europe and steamers go very rapidly. Spain is a strange land ! When we went into the first room I saw a number of people with shaven heads. I guessed that these were either grandees or soldiers because they do shave their heads. I thought the behaviour of the High Chancellor who led me by the hand, extremely strange. He thrust me into a little room and said : 'Sit there, and if you persist in calling yourself King Ferdinand, I'll knock the inclination out of you !' But knowing that this was only to try me I answered in the negative, whereupon the Chancellor hit me twice on the back and it hurt so that I almost cried out, but restrained myself, remembering that this is the custom of chivalry on receiving any exalted dignity, for customs of chivalry persist in Spain to this day. When I was alone I decided to occupy myself with affairs of state. I discovered that Spain and China were one and the same country, and it is only through ignorance that they are considered to be different kingdoms. I recommend everyone to try and write Spain on a bit of paper and it will always turn out China. But I was particularly distressed by an event which will take place to-morrow. To-morrow at seven o'clock a strange phenomenon will occur ; the earth will fall on the moon. The celebrated English chemist, Wellington, has written about it. I must confess that I experience a tremor at my heart when I reflect upon the extreme softness and fragility of the moon. You see the moon is, generally, made in Hamburg and very badly made, too. I am surprised that England hasn't taken notice of it. It was made by a lame cooper, and it is evident that the fool had no idea what a moon should be. He put in tarred cord and one part of olive oil ; and that is why there is such a fearful stench all over the world that one has to stop one's nose. And that's how it is that the moon is such a soft globe that man cannot live on it and that nothing lives there but noses. And it is for that very reason that we can't see our noses, because they all live in the moon. And when I reflected that the earth is a heavy body and when it falls it may grind our noses to powder I was so overcome by uneasiness that, putting on my shoes and stockings, I hastened to the hall of the Imperial Council to give orders to the police not to allow the earth to fall on the moon. The grandees with shaven heads whom I found in great numbers in the hall of the Imperial Council were very intelligent people, and when I said : 'Gentlemen, let us save the moon, for the earth is trying to fall on it !' they all rushed to carry out my sovereign wishes, and several climbed up the walls to try and get at the moon : but at that moment the High Chancellor walked in. Seeing him they all ran in different directions. I, as King, alone remained. But to my amazement the Chancellor struck me with his stick and drove me back to my room ! So great is the power of national customs in Spain ! "

IV

There are two more stories Gogol had written about the same period : *The Nose* and *The Carriage*.*

As to the first of them, its subject might have been indirectly suggested to him by those passages of Sterne's *Tristram Shandy* (published in a Russian translation in 1804-07) which deal with noses. Besides, there existed a whole "nosological" literature at that time, and Gogol seems to have been much attracted by various anecdotes and jokes about this part of the human body.** The hero of the mentioned story is a certain Major Kovalyov—a self-satisfied and empty *parvenu* whose ambitions, rank and position in society are suddenly endangered owing to the trifling fact that one fine morning he awakes without a nose on his face. Thrown out of all ordinary conditions of life, he embarks upon an

* He was then doing also some journalistic work (in connection with Pushkin's *Sovremennik*) of which his *Petersburg Notes* (1836) are very witty and vivid—especially his comparison of Petersburg and Moscow. Also his *Movement of our Journalistic Literature*, of 1834–5 is interesting.

** He himself had a long and ugly nose. But there were also subconscious reasons.

anxious search for his nose which has deserted him and which wanders about Petersburg, leading an independent existence. Kovalyov's encounters with his own nose and various misunderstandings which result from his anxious and extremely delicate errand give Gogol ample opportunity of displaying not only all his gift for the nonsensical, but a good deal of biting satire as well. Yet in spite of its many excellent passages, the final impression of the story is that of confusion, of a too sophisticated attempt to imitate the absurd logic of dreams. But what might be entirely convincing if treated on the plane of a dream, is artistically less convincing when presented outside that plane. As a matter of fact, Gogol did first conceive the whole story simply as a dream. Its first Russian title was *Son* (*i.e.*, A Dream). But probably seduced by the play of words, Gogol reversed this into *Nos* which is the Russian equivalent for the nose. Then he took all the nonsensical logic of the "dream" and applied it to the waking Petersburg reality in such a way as to mix the two planes, making out of the whole thing a grotesque puzzle the key to which is to be found not so much in the artistic as in the psycho-analytical kind of symbolism.

The Carriage again is, in spite of its anecdotic subject-matter, a perfect thing. It reminds one of Chehov—of the humorous Chehov at his best. Its detached and gay tone is perhaps due to the fact that Gogol transfers us once more to his beloved South. The story is compact, written with extreme economy, without a single digression from the essentials. Its humour and veiled irony are spontaneous throughout, with a perfect balance between the comicality of the situations and that of the characters.

But while talking of Gogol's stories, we must lay stress on his most important Petersburg story—*The Cloak*, although, together with the fragment, *Rome*, it belongs to a later period (1839-40). We need not waste many words on his *Rome*, which is full of rhetorical superlatives and blazing *clichés*. Gogol's single observations, his vivid description of the Roman Carnival, as well as of a few common types, are nevertheless excellent. Apart from this, the fragment itself, which was printed by Pogodin (in his *Moskvityanin*, 1842) against Gogol's wish and in payment of debts, has a certain biographic interest.*

The Cloak, on the other hand, is of a different order both by its subject and by the influence it had upon the subsequent period of Russian literature. The main character of this story, a certain Akaky Akakievitch, is a second Popprischin, *i.e.*, a poor down-trodden official. Yet

* The young prince's attitude towards Paris and Rome, towards the French and Italians, is that of Gogol himself.

while the imaginary King of Spain dared to protest at least in his fancy, Akaky was so maimed by fate that he was incapable of craving for anything that went beyond the routine of his miserable existence. He was one of those beings who are meek, good and industrious out of weakness. Being entirely resigned, he felt even happy in his own way ; at any rate, he was hardly aware of the degradation of his own life—the life of a half-starved copying clerk sitting year after year at the same table, in the same duty, as if he had been born into the world " ready-made, as he was—uniform, bald patch and all ". His chiefs treated him with despotism, the porters with spite, and the younger clerks with merciless irony. Only when their jokes at his expense became too rude did he occasionally flare up for a moment—like a sickly animal which had been kicked : " ' Leave me alone ! Why will you worry me ? ' And there was a strange quality both in the words and the tone in which they were uttered ; a quality that aroused pity." Otherwise Akaky was too much absorbed in his mechanical drudgery to pay any attention to his tormentors.

" No man was so absorbed in his work as Akaky Akakievitch. It is so little to say that he worked with zeal—he worked with love. The act of copying papers opened to him a world of his own—a pleasant world full of variety. An expression of pleasure flitted across his face when he settled down to his task, and when he came to his favourite letters he smiled and blinked his eyes and moved his lips so that one could almost tell from his face what letters his pen was forming . . . Besides copying, nothing else existed for him. He never gave a thought to his dress, and his uniform was no longer green, but of a rusty mealy hue. His collar was low and narrow, and though he had not a long neck it seemed unnaturally long, like the necks of the plaster kittens foreign vendors carry on trays on their heads. And something was always sticking to his coat, such as a piece of straw, or thread ; and he possessed a wonderful knack of passing a window at the exact moment when the inmate was pitching some rubbish into the street, so that he invariably went about with bits of melon and pumpkin rind lodged in the brim of his hat. . . . When he reached home he would sit down to the table and eat his soup, and a piece of mutton and onion, scarcely aware of their taste, together with the flies and anything the Lord cared to send at the time. His stomach filled, he would rise from the table, take out an ink-pot and begin copying the papers he had brought home. If there chanced to be no papers to copy for the office, he would copy one for himself, particularly if the document happened to be remarkable, not so much by its contents as by the fact of its being addressed to some person of importance . . . Having written to his heart's content he would go to bed with a smile on his face at the prospect of the morrow. What would he be given to copy to-morrow ? "

But in the middle of winter a calamity befell him : his worn-out overcoat, or the " dressing-jacket " as the office wits called it, got so thin and in places even torn that it could no longer protect him from the fierce northern winds. With much reluctance Akaky decided to consult his old acquaintance about the matter, the one-eyed and eternally drunken tailor, Petrovitch, who lived in the same house. After endless diplomatic precautions he broached the delicate subject : " It's like this, Petrovitch . . . the overcoat, the cloth . . . you see everywhere it is quite strong ; it's a little dusty, and looks as though it were old, but it is new and it is only in one place just a little . . . on the back, and just a little worn on one shoulder and on this shoulder, too, a little . . . do you see ? That's all and it isn't much work . . . ."

As if on purpose, Petrovitch happened to be sober on that day. After a thorough inspection of the overcoat he shook his head and passed the verdict which made Akaky's heart sink : " No, it can't be repaired ; a wretched garment ! " But something must have been wrong with him, too ; for he suggested the incredible idea that Akaky should order an expensive new cloak, and a fashionable one ; with silver-plated buckles, with a marten collar, and various other adornments. Akaky considered the very thought of it too ridiculous and went away with the decision to return another time—when he would be sure to find Petrovitch in a less sober state. He called at such a moment, but although drunk, Petrovitch mumbled again about ordering a new cloak and refused to have anything to do with Akaky's dilapidated garment. And again Akaky went home in despondence. Yet the prospect of a new cloak got hold of him. At first as an idea, then as a temptation, then as a vision, and at last as an obsession which overpowered the whole of his mind to such an extent that soon he could think of nothing else. The only ambition in his old age was to scrape enough money together and order a fashionable cloak. But how and where could he get the money? While puzzling over the dilemma, he resolved " to cut down his ordinary expenses for at least a year. He could forego his evening tea, do without candles ; if he had to work in the evening he could always go in to his landlady's ; he would have to step lightly over the stones in the street, walk almost on tip-toe, thus to save shoe-leather ;

he would send his linen to the wash less often ; and, in order to keep it clean as long as possible, he could take his under-clothes off in the evening and sit in his old, worn cotton dressing-gown . . . He found it difficult to accustom himself to these privations at first, but by degrees he grew used to them and all went well ; he even resigned himself to evenings of hunger, having in consolation a certain spiritual satisfaction in the contemplation of his future cloak. During those days his life seemed to have grown richer ; he might have become married ; it seemed as though some other person was always with him, some dear friend with whom he trod the path of life, and this friend was none other than his future cloak, padded with thick wadding and lined with a strong lasting lining. He was more animated, more resolute, like a man with a definite purpose in view. Doubt and uncertainty disappeared from his face and his manner ; a fire was occasionally seen in his eye, and the most daring audacious thoughts floated about in his brain. Could he not rise to a marten collar ? The very thought reduced him to a state of blankness, once nearly causing him to make a mistake in his writing, but he recovered himself with an " Oh, dear ! ' and made the sign of the cross."

Luck smiled on him. He managed to obtain some unexpected money which he added to the small sum already saved ; he also came to satisfactory terms with Petrovitch. The great day arrived at last : the magnificent cloak was ready—true, with a cat-skin instead of marten, but the cat-skin had been so well chosen that at a distance everyone would take it for real marten. And so Akaky walked along to the office, happy and proud as an emperor. The smart new cloak on his shoulders made him smile with inner satisfaction. And then the surprise, the consternation even, produced by the cloak in the office ! For the first time in his life Akaky felt that he had suddenly become somebody. He was congratulated, talked about, admired. And what is more, one of the higher officials decided there and then to celebrate the great event by an evening party. Akaky joined the party, drank a little too much ; and pleased with the cloak, with himself, with the whole world, he walked home late at night. After having passed a few deserted streets, he had to cross a lonely square which he did with certain trepidation.

" The cloak is mine ! " suddenly thundered a voice, while a ruffian seized him by the collar.

Akaky opened his mouth to protest, to call for help, but a big fist shut it in good time. He felt his gorgeous cloak being torn from his shoulders. Then somebody kicked him. He tumbled in the snow, lost consciousness. When he came to his senses again there was no trace left either of the cloak or of the ruffians. The despair nearly drove him mad. He tried to recover his cloak through the authorities, but without success. And after all the trouble, particularly after his visit to a new-fledged " person of consequence "—a general—who nearly frightened him out of his wits by sheer self-importance, Akaky fell ill and died, talking even in delirium of the thieves and of his beloved overcoat.

V

It is interesting that this story, too, is based upon an anecdote which Gogol heard at a tea-party in 1834. One of the guests related how a certain minor official, being passionately fond of sport, cut all his expenses in such a way as to save enough money to buy a fine sporting rifle. He bought the rifle, but on the very first day of his sport he dropped it quite by chance into a river. The poor man fell ill and would probably have lost his reason had not his comrades made a collection and presented him with another rifle.

This anecdote about the sporting official and his responsive comrades is in itself rather touching and delightful. Yet, as V. Rozanov has already pointed out, Gogol transformed even this subject into a gloomy story permeated both with pity and scorn. While the original anecdote shows nothing but pleasant features—a passionate love of sport, the kindness of colleagues, Gogol at once conceived the whole matter in such a way as to proclaim the official a " good-natured animal " (in the first draft) and emphasize the " senseless brutality " of the chaffing young clerks, the snobbery of the higher officials, and the hardness of human beings in general.* Once more, Gogol picked up as many negative data of real life as he possibly could, condensed them, and grouped them together in such a way as to make the pitiable scribe, Akaky,

* In the final version of *The Cloak* we read this somewhat false-sounding passage which was probably interpolated after the story had been finished : " A newly-appointed young man, imitating the others, began to make fun of him, but he pulled himself up suddenly as though touched to the quick, and since then everything was changed for him, and he saw Akaky Akakievitch in a new light. Some supernatural power drew him away from his comrades, whom he had taken for decent, well-bred fellows. Long afterwards, in the merriest of moments, he recalled the little clerk with the bald patch on his head and his touching words, ' Leave me alone ! Why will you worry me ? ' And beneath these words he seemed to hear the refrain, " Am I not your brother ? ' And the poor young man would cover his face and shudder at the age he lived in, when a man was so inhuman and there was so much senseless brutality in his so-called refined good-breeding—oh, God ! even a man whom the world regarded as upright and honourable." These few lines, whose rhetorical flavour does not harmonize with the general tone of the story, are responsible for many notes of pity in subsequent Russian Literature.

not only a haunting parody of man, but also a symbol and an accusation of life as a whole.

Yet the story itself is a literary masterpiece. The manner in which Gogol enlarges the insignificant theme of the stolen overcoat into a great human tragedy is admirable. And again he knows how to strengthen its effect by his usual mixture of the tragic with the comic, a mixture which we feel in his very tone. It is the incongruity between the tone of a grinning impersonator on the one hand, and a pitying observer on the other, that strengthens the grotesqueness of the story. The more pitiful the matter he is dealing with the more comic becomes his tone. And as if laughing at last over his own pity, Gogol makes the delirious Akaky utter oaths such as caused his old landlady to cross herself, and then he suddenly rounds up the whole subject with the grotesque idea of Akaky's "ghost" stealing cloaks in the streets of Petersburg.

Although Gogol had not been the first to introduce the poor degraded official into Russian literature, his *Cloak* had a considerable influence upon that "natural" school out of which came the great Russian realists. The story itself shows indeed some of his most striking qualities, above all his great capacity for significant trifles through which he always takes reality by surprise, as it were. He displays in it all the art of *indiscretion about small things :* as if he were peeping at men and objects through a keyhole, every now and then significantly winking at the reader. His very irony is of a " peeping " kind. And again he does not describe or analyze reality : he dissociates it, and from all the dissociated elements he puts together only those which he needs in order to express his own subjective vision rather than a likeness of life. And as usual, he achieves this by a careful selection, by a complete change of proportions and finally by combinations of apparently incongruous elements which he reconstructs in such a way as to make them convincing owing to their very grotesqueness. He often reminds one of the painter, Goya, who also was a master in intensifying things into spooks of things, and real people into spooks of people.

Had Gogol's imagination been more self-supporting he might have become a kind of Russian E. T. W. Hoffmann on a big scale. But owing to his lack of invention, he always had to lean on external facts, on collected materials and anecdotes, and even on other people's themes. " I never created anything out of mere imagination," he says in his *Author's Confession.* " Only in those things was I successful which I took from reality and which were based on the data I knew. I could fathom a man then only when

I had seen all the minutest details of his exterior. Yet I never *painted* a portrait by simply copying it. I *created* portraits, but I created them on the ground of consideration rather than on that of mere imagination. The more details I had seen and considered, the better were my productions. My mind is in this respect thoroughly Russian, that is, a mind capable of deriving rather than of inventing."

Gogol's art is, in fact, the result of an utterly romantic temper combined with the cold observation of a collector or of a scientific investigator. And the more abundant his collected data, the easier it is for him to weave out of them the pattern he needs. Hence his innate inquisitiveness even about the most casual things. This was one of his passions. He himself acknowledges in his *Dead Souls* that even as a child he used to scrutinize and fathom every person, every trifle he came across. " It made no difference to me whether it were a little village, a poor, wretched distant town, a hamlet, or a suburb, my inquisitive childish eyes discovered much that was of interest in it. Nothing escaped my fresh, alert attention, and poking my nose out of my cart, I stared at the novel cut of some coat, and at the wooden chests of nails, of sulphur, yellow in the distance, of raisins, and of soap, of which I caught glimpses through the door of a grocer's shop, together with jars of stale Moscow sweets. I stared, too, at the infantry officer who had been cast by fate from God knows what province into the boredom of this remote district, and at the dealer in his long overcoat, flying by in his racing droshky, and in my thoughts I was carried along with them into their poor lives. If a local official walked by, at once I fell to speculating where he was going, whether it was to spend the evening with some fellow-clerk, or straight home to lounge for half-an-hour on the steps till the twilight had turned to darkness ; and then to sit down to an early supper with his mother, his wife, his wife's sister and all his family, and what their talk would be about, while a serf-girl in necklaces, or a boy in thick, short jacket brought in, but only after the soup, a tallow candle in a candlestick that had seen long years of service in the household. As I drove up to some landowner's village, I looked with curiosity at the tall, narrow, wooden belfry, or at the spacious old church of dark wood. Through the green of the trees the red roofs and white chimneys of the owner's house gleamed alluringly in the distance, and I waited with impatience for a gap through the gardens that screened it on both sides, that I might get a full view of its exterior, and from it I tried to guess what the owner himself was like, whether he was a fat man, or whether he had sons, or a full set of six daughters, with ringing girlish laughter and games, and the youngest sister , of course a beauty, and whether they had black eyes, or whether he was a merry fellow himself, or, gloomy as the last days of September, looked at the calendar and talked about the rye and wheat, while the young people sat bored."*

Gogol's capacity for patient and cold observation contrasts very strangely with the nervous heat and verve of his temperament ; yet in a way, it is precisely this combination which often makes his writing so unique and elusive. It also gives a clue to the curious fact that, in spite of all the apparent spontaneity of his works, Gogol wrote them perhaps more self-consciously than any other great writer of his time. However spontaneous his first drafts might have been, he never trusted things jotted down in the first impulse of inspiration ; for years he went on remodelling them, even after they had been printed, re-writing, burning, starting them again, without ever being pleased with the result. As N. V. Berg records, Gogol confessed (in 1850) that he usually made and re-copied each of his works eight times. At first he put down everything just as it came to him. But after this he considered most thoroughly each sentence, each word even, all the time

* It may be of interest that Gogol has endowed with this very quality the main character of the *Dead Souls*, Chichikov.

collecting and adding new details, new shades and aspects. And together with this, he always had recourse to those artistic means at his disposal which he found most efficient in his strife with actuality or with himself. Humour, satire, anger, moral indictments—they all were welcomed as long as he could turn them into good weapons. And in some way or other, he always did turn them into weapons.

Chapter Five

GOGOL THE PLAYWRIGHT

I

A careful perusal of Gogol's early stories can easily convince one that he had written them with the vivacity and the vision of a born actor. The theatrical vein was, and remained in a way, one of the dominant features of his genius. Hence it was natural that he should try his strength in drama as well. He conceived in fact several plays soon after his first literary success. Already in 1832 he had begun at least two comedies : *The Vladimir Order*, and *The Wooers* (later published as *The Marriage*).

The subject of the *Vladimir Order* is an ambitious and dishonest official whose great aim is to obtain the Vladimir Order ; but seeing this aim frustrated by intrigues, he goes mad and imagines he himself is the Order of Vladimir. Gogol's intention in this piece was to give a biting satire of the Russian bureaucracy. But as there was no hope that the censor would ever allow such a work to be performed or published, his inspiration was all the time hampered by the thought of possible consequences. "I did not write to you that I went mad over the subject for a comedy," he wrote to Pogodin (on February 20th, 1833). "It stuck in my mind all the time while I was in Moscow, on my journey, and also after I had arrived here (in Petersburg), but so far I have not finished anything. Not so long ago its content began to shape itself, even its title was already written on thick white paper—*Vladimir of the Third Class*; and how much malice, laughter and salt there was in it! . . . But I suddenly stopped, seeing that my pen began to stumble over passages of which the censor would not approve for anything on earth. And what is the use of a play which cannot be produced at all: a play lives only on the stage? A play without the stage is like a soul without the body. . . . The only thing that remains to me is to write so as not to offend even the last police-officer. But what again is the use of a comedy which is without truth and without malice?"

It was chiefly for this reason that Gogol gave up finishing his *Vladimir*, of which there exist only three separate and rather biting fragments (in their final version—made some time between 1837 and 42): *The Servants' Room*, *The Lawsuit*, and *The Fragment.** Yet his dramatic vein, once aroused, could not be suppressed so easily. The malice and laughter that had been intended for his *Vladimir* he soon embodied in another work called *The Revizor*—the best and the most celebrated comedy of the Russian repertory. At the same time he was trying to make out of his *Wooers* a harmless but extremely vivid play which however appeared in its final version only in 1842 under the title, *The Marriage.*

II

This exquisite comedy, brimming with laughter and movement, is a dramatized anecdote in which Gogol confronts the world of the *chinovniks* (officials) with that of the conservative Russian merchants. It is based on a " quite incredible happening "—on that nonsense of life which up to a certain line remains highly comical owing precisely to its casualness, to its lack of all logic or significance. Gogol, who is particularly fond of tackling the nonsensical side of human existence, here remains all the time on that plane of the comic where life passes into the parody of life.

* The theme of the ambitious official who goes mad was used by Gogol later on for his *Madman's Diary,* in which he split the hero of the *Vladimir* into two separate characters : Poprischin and his chief.

The play itself has no love-intrigue, no love-scenes. Both love and marriage are treated in it ironically : only as a kind of commercial contract in which the dowry is of far greater importance than its appendage—the bride. The plot is highly humorous and simple. A certain official, Podkolyossin, is persuaded by a professional matchmaker to woo a rich merchant's daughter. Owing partly to her efforts and partly to those of a hot-headed friend of his, the phlegmatic Podkolyossin is seduced by the dowry and decides to have a look at his possible spouse, Agafya, herself. He is favoured by luck : Agafya prefers him to all other candidates. But at the very height of his enthusiasm over the prospects of a married life, he suddenly becomes frightened of such a change in his existence. And what is worse, this fear overwhelms him before the wedding and in the room of his happy bride, Agafya. Finding no other retreat open, he jumps through the window and escapes probably with a broken rib, but without a wife. He chooses, in short, the lesser evil.

The chief virtue of this piece lies in its compactness and its unique dialogue, which is doomed to lose its flavour in any translation whatsoever. Like most Russian comedies of that time, *The Marriage* is based on French tradition with particular leanings towards Molière. However,

Gogol's humour is coarser, and he indulges even more in funny illogical motives and associations than Molière himself. The action of the play is quick and full of unexpected situations. But while in the *Evenings* Gogol's use of the comic is chiefly in the situations, here the comicality of the characters and that of the situations go hand in hand. The scene when the lazy Podkolyossin arrives at Agafya's house and finds there five other competitors, all of them brought together by the zeal of the same match-maker, is particularly amusing. Equally good is the delineation of other types—a few dexterous touches on the part of Gogol are enough to make them alive. If properly acted, *The Marriage* provokes one continuous scream of laughter.

Although this play had a considerable influence on Ostrovsky—the greatest Russian playwright of the generation which came after Gogol—it looks like a relaxation rather than anything else on the part of its author. There are no hidden tears in the laughter aroused by it. Even the satire is entirely drowned in the comedy. The only thing that may perhaps arouse at times our suspicion is the fact that Gogol's laughter is here just a little too loud.

Of an entirely different range and quality is, however, Gogol's *Revizor*. This is no longer a merely exhilarating comedy, but a satire full of gall and hidden indignation. It is saturated with all that " malice, laughter and salt " which he had to suppress when giving up the plan for his *Vladimir.* And as to its technique, it is a work made of one piece. Everything in it is inevitable. Each situation, each figure, is an organic part of the whole. The play abounds in grinning irony and indirect indictments ; yet being moral in the best sense as all true art always is, it is not in the least moralizing ; there is not a single puppet spluttering out " ideas " and moral recipes. Apart from this, each character speaks a language of his own and, as in *The Marriage*, the comicality of the characters strengthens that of the situations. Together with Griboyedov's *Gore ot Uma* (The Mischief of being Clever),* *The Revizor* belongs to the favourite plays of the Russian stage. And it certainly deserves this honour.

III

Gogol began to write his *Revizor* in 1834. The play appeared in print in 1836, and its final version was published in 1842. Its motive is

* An English translation of this comedy in verse by Sir Bernard Pares has appeared in *The Slavonic Review*, Vol. III, Nos. 7 and 8.

almost as old as comedy itself, and Gogol's own variation of a traditional theme was partly suggested to him by Pushkin and partly by other works of a similar kind, Russian and foreign. Kvitka's *Newcomer from the Capital* (1827), for instance, deals (rather clumsily) with almost the same motive ; and a thorough scrutiny could discover in Gogol's masterpiece situations reminding us of Molière, or of Corneille's *Menteur*. These resemblances are, of course, casual. But even if they were not so, the main point is not whence an author gets his motives, but whether he can make them his own. In literature one is allowed to steal as much as one can really appropriate ; and whenever Gogol takes anything from others he always knows how to make it his own.

The genesis of *The Revizor* is due to an anecdote told by Pushkin of how he himself had been mistaken in Nizhny Novgorod for a high official from Petersburg who had arrived incognito in order to inspect the order of the town. Such a *qui-pro-quo* is in itself only funny. Gogol's imagination, however, transmuted also this incident in such a way as to make it a pretext for showing the whole of Russian life in its most pessimistic aspect—under the mask of fun and laughter. The action of the play takes place in a provincial town whose *gorodnichy* (a kind of town-governor), Anton Antonovitch Dmookhanovsky,* is privately informed by a friend that the revizor, or Inspector-General, from Petersburg will visit his town in strict incognito. Thunderstruck by such news, the gorodnichy summons to his house the chief officials of the town, all of whom are prostrate with fear that their transgressions may perhaps be discovered and duly punished. The absurdest and most illogical conjectures are made with regard to the revizor's arrival. The personal situation of each of them looks so serious indeed that they all try to devise various self-protective measures. The gorodnichy initiates even the local postmaster, Ivan Kuzmich, into the whole business : " Well, I'm no coward, but I *am* just a little uncomfortable. The shop-keepers and townspeople bother me. It seems I am unpopular with them ; but the Lord knows, if I've blackmailed anybody I've done it without a trace of ill-feeling. I even think (*buttonholes him*

* His description is an example of that precision with which Gogol visualizes his characters : " A man who has grown old in the State service—in his opinion a smart official. He wears an air of dignified respectability, but is by no means incorruptible. He speaks to the point, generally avoiding extremes, but sometimes launching into an argument. His features are harsh and stern, like those of a *chinovnik* who has worked his way up from the lowest rank. His coarse and ill-educated nature causes him to pass with rapidity from fear to joy, and from servility to arrogance. He is dressed in uniform, with loops and facings, and wears Hessian boots with spurs."

and takes him aside)—I even think there will be some sort of complaint drawn up against me. . . . Why should we have a revizor at all ? Look here, Ivan Kuzmich, don't you think you could slightly open every letter which comes in and goes out of your office, and read it (for the public benefit, you know) to see if it contains any kind of information against me or only correspondence ? If it is all right, you can seal it up again ; or simply deliver the letter opened."

" Oh, I know that game " answers the good-natured post-master. " Don't teach me *that!* I do it from pure curiosity, not as a precaution. I am death on knowing what's going on in the world. And they're very interesting to read, I can tell you ! Now and then you come across a love-letter, with bits of beautiful language, and so edifying. . . ."

But here two worthies, Bobchinsky and Dobchinsky, rush in with rather exciting news. They had seen in the local hotel a young *chinovnik* from Petersburg who was casting very inquisitive looks at everything, even at what people were eating. They found out that the name of the elegant young man was Khlestakov and that he had been staying there for a fortnight under very mysterious circumstances. Who else could he be but the revizor ? Both of them are ready to swear he is the revizor himself.

The gorodnichy's panic and confusion increase. On hearing, however, that the dreaded person is still young, he decides to make a professional *tour de force* : to bribe him, and cautiously invite him to be his guest. Trusting in God's mercy, he sets off to the hotel, having first given a few necessary instructions, such as these : " The police-lieutenant—he is tall, so he's to stand on the bridge—that will give a good effect. Then the old fence near the bootmaker's must be pulled down at once and scattered about, and a post stuck up with a wisp of straw, so as to look like building operations. The more litter there is, the more it will show the Governor's zeal and activity. . . . Good God ! though, I forgot that about forty cart-loads of rubbish have been shot behind that fence. What a dirty town this is ! No matter where you put a monument, or even a paling, they collect all kinds of rubbish from the devil knows where, and upset it there ! . . . And if the newly-come chinovnik asks any of the officials if they are contented, they're to say : 'Perfectly, your Honour,' and if anybody is *not* contented, I'll give him something afterwards to be discontented about . . . (*heaves a sigh*)—ah-h-h ! I am a sinner—a terrible sinner ! Heaven only grant that I may soon get quit of the matter, and then I'll give such a taper for a thank-offering as has never been given before ! I'll levy three *puds* * of wax from every merchant for it! . . . And if he asks why the hospital chapel has not been built for which the money was voted five years ago, they must mind and say that it began to be built, but was burnt down. Why, I drew up a report about it. But of course some idiot is sure to forget, and let out that the building was never begun. . . . And tell Derzhimorda that he's not to give such free play to his fists; guilty or innocent, he makes them all see stars, in the cause of public order. . . ."

The instructions speak for themselves. But while the zealous gorodnichy goes to bribe the imaginary revizor, Khlestakov himself is in terrible straits. To begin with, he is a petty official of the lowest grade, and in addition an irresponsible, naïve charlatan who has lost all his money at cards while on the way to his father's estate. His affairs are so bad, indeed, that he is already refused meals on credit and is even threatened with gaol unless he settles his accounts. Hungry and out of spirits he actually expects to be arrested—he expects this at the very moment when the trembling gorodnichy enters his room. They stare at each other in trepidation.

GORODNICHY (*plucking up courage a little, and saluting deferentially*): I hope you are well, sir!

KHLESTAKOV (*bows*): My respects to you, sir!

* A *pud*—36 lbs.

GORODNICHY: Excuse my intruding. . . . It is my duty as chief magistrate of this town, to take all due measures to prevent travellers and persons of rank from suffering any inconvenience.

Khlestakov thinks this is only a polite pretext for arresting him and begins to vent his indignation by accusing the innkeeper who sends him up " beef as hard as a board. And the soup—the devil only knows *what* he'd mixed up with it: I was obliged to pitch it out of the window. He starves me the whole day. . . . And the tea's so peculiar; it smells of fish and nothing else! Why then should I . . . a *fine* idea, indeed!"

The gorodnichy takes Khlestakov's complaint for an accusation of the order in the town and answers in a faltering voice: " I assure you it's not my fault, really. I always get good beef from the market. The Kholmogori drovers bring it, and they are sober and well-principled people. I am sure I don't know where he gets it from. But if anything is wrong . . . allow me to suggest that you come with me and get other quarters."

" No, that I will *not*. I know what 'other quarters' means," shouts Khlestakov, who again interprets the gorodnichy's words in his own way. " And pray, what right have you—how dare you? . . . Why, I . . . I'm a Government official at Petersburg . . . (*defiantly*). Yes, . . . I . . . I . . . (*aggressively*), that for you and your governorship together ! I'll not go with you. I'll go straight to the Minister. (*Bangs his fist on the table*). Who are *you*, pray, who are you ? "

GORODNICHY (*starting, and shaking all over*): Have pity on me ! Don't ruin me ! I have a wife and small children ! Don't make me a miserable man ! . . . It was only inexperience, I swear, only my inexperience ! And insufficient means ! Judge for yourself—the salary I get is not enough for tea and sugar. And if I *have* taken any bribes, they were very little ones—something for the table or a coat or two. . . . As for the sergeant's widow, who took to shop-keeping—whom they say I had flogged—it's slander, I swear it's slander. My enemies invented it—they're the kind of people who are ready to murder me in cold blood."

In the end, however, things turn out quite favourably for the gorodnichy, and even more so for Khlestakov, who instead of being arrested is offered money and hospitality. The would-be revizor is solemnly taken to the gorodnichy's house, where he is feasted, admired, idolized. He is led about the town and shown various institutions. All the representatives of the local bureaucracy consider it their duty to introduce themselves to him—one by one, to see whether there will be any orders on his part, to give him bribes, as well as to slander, secretly, of course, their colleagues and their best friends. Khlestakov, however, is the last man to bother about the real meaning of things and events. He enjoys himself, eats, drinks and boasts. In all this he is full of spontaneity and relish, particularly when he boasts about himself. And he does so with no evil intent, but in the manner of a Russian Tartarin who lies with temperament, even with inspiration because he is the first to believe all he says. His fancies contrive the reality in such a way as to give him at least a moment's illusion of his own importance. Khlestakov is, in short, another Poprischin—Ferdinand VII, without Poprischin's tragedy and madness. He is just an irresponsible braggart with the brains and egotism of a child. Seeing all these provincial worthies staring at him with wondering and open mouths, he simply cannot help displaying before them his own imaginary grandeur. His house is, of course, the first in Petersburg. He gives balls and dinners, the magnificence of which surpasses all description. " On the table, for instance, is a water melon that costs several hundred roubles. The soup comes straight from Paris by steamer in the tureen : there's nothing in the world to be compared with its flavour ! I go to a ball every day. We have our whist-clubs there, too : the Foreign Minister, the French Ambassador, the German Ambassador and myself. . . ."

He makes, moreover, love to his host's wife and daughter. To the latter he even becomes engaged. The gorodnichy's excessive fear thus changes into such joy that he almost loses his head. Khlestakov, on the other hand, abandons himself to the course of events without giving a single thought either to their reasons or their possible consequences. The only man who begins to feel somewhat uneasy is his shrewd serf who travels with him. Guessing that the good people must have mistaken his master for somebody else, he urges him to get away as soon as possible. And so, having received considerable " loans " not only from the local chinovniks, but also from the merchants who came to complain of the gorodnichy's misdeeds, Khlestakov makes off—" at a moment's notice, but for a day only " —with his accumulated pleasant memories and money. But before leaving the hospitable town, he posts a letter to a friend of his, with an account of all that has happened to him. Meanwhile, the gorodnichy's triumph over fate and over his " enemies " reaches its zenith. His own daughter betrothed to such a great personage ! It is almost past belief, and yet it is true. Swelling with pride and self-importance, he summons the merchants who dared to complain of him. His rage knows no limits. Carried away by moral indignation, he accuses them even of utter lack of gratitude : " You complained of me? But who was it winked at your jobbery when you built the bridge and charged twenty thousand for less than a hundred roubles' worth of wood? It was I, you goatsbeards ! Have you forgotten that? If I had rounded on you, I could have sent you to Siberia ! What say you to *that*—eh? I have a good mind to . . . but no (*waves his hand condescendingly*). There, may the Lord forgive you ! Enough—I bear no malice ; only beware and mind your P's and Q's ! For I am not giving my daughter to any ordinary gentleman ; so see that the wedding presents are . . . you understand? And don't flatter yourselves you can put me off with your dried fish or sugar-loaves. . . . There, now, you can go, and the Lord be with you."

The news of his daughter's engagement rapidly spreads in the town. All respectable citizens hurry to congratulate the mighty gorodnichy and his spouse. The gorodnichy's residence is soon filled with radiant faces, with exclamations of joy, with insinuating compliments. But the mighty ones feel already so exalted, so high above the level of their fellow-citizens that they do not consider it necessary even to hide their disgust with such provincials as their own friends.

"We intend to live in Petersburg now," says the gorodnichy's wife. "*Here*, there's such an air, I must say . . . it's really too rustic ! . . . I find it excessively disagreeable . . . my husband, too . . . he will get a general's rank there ! "

But soon the postmaster appears. He comes out of breath and holding a letter in his hand—the very one that Khlestakov had posted before his departure. The good man had duly opened it and naturally was puzzled by its contents.

"Here's an astounding thing happened," he exclaims. "The chinovnik we took to be the revizor is *not* a revizor."

The news has the effect of a thunderbolt. Yet it is too unexpected to be taken in at once. The stupid postmaster may be only joking. But here the bearer of the unexpected tidings begins to read the letter, which runs as follows : "I hasten to let you know, my dear Tryapichkin, all about my adventures. On the way an infantry captain cleared me out completely, so that the innkeeper wanted to send me to gaol ; when all of a sudden, owing to my Petersburg get-up and appearance, the whole town took me for the Governor-General. So now I am living at the gorodnichy's. I do just as I please ; I flirt madly with his wife and daughter, but I can't settle which to begin with. Do you remember how hard up we were, how we dined at other's folks' expense, and how the pastry-cook once pitched me out neck and crop, because I had put some tarts I had eaten down to the account of the King of England? It is quite a different state of things now! They all lend me as much money as ever I please. They are an awful set of originals—you would die of laughing if you saw them! You write articles, I know: bring these people in. First and foremost, there's the gorodnichy—he's as stupid as a mule. . . ."

And so on. Every member of the wonderful company gets a suitable label taken from the zoological world. While the letter is being read the scales fall from their eyes; the artificial mist disperses and the barren truth stares them in the face. The blinded gorodnichy himself is compelled at last to see it.

"How could I?" he begins to shout as if in a fit of madness. "There is not such another old blockhead as I am. I must be in my dotage, idiot of a mutton-head that I am. . . . Thirty years have I been in the service; not a tradesman or contractor could cheat me; rogue after rogue have I overreached, sharpers and rascals have I hooked, that were ready to rob the whole universe! Three governors-general I've duped! . . . Pooh! What are governors-general? (*with a contemptuous wave of the hand*). They're not worth talking about. . . . Taking an icicle, a rag, for a man of rank ! And now he is rattling along the road with his bells and telling the whole world the story ! "

However, a worse blow follows. While the gorodnichy curses his own stupidity, a gendarme enters and announces to him in a stern voice :

" The Inspector-General sent by Imperial command has arrived and requests your attendance at once. He awaits you in the inn."

The whole assembly remains as if petrified. Here the curtain falls.

IV

Such is the skeleton of this comedy, with regard to which Gogol said later, in his *Author's Confession* : " I saw that in my former works I laughed for nothing, uselessly, without knowing why. If it is necessary to laugh, then let us laugh at that which really deserves to be laughed at by all. In my *Revizor* I decided to gather in one place and deride all that is bad in Russia, all the evils which are being perpetrated in those places where the utmost rectitude is required from man."

Corruption, snobbery, stupidity, malice—the whole compendium of vices which could be found in a stagnant provincial existence is focussed in *The Revizor* and whipped with merciless laughter. Gogol never moralizes nor does he indulge in direct indictments. He does not even pretend to swing the whip in his own hands, but makes his characters whip themselves without knowing it, as it were, especially when they talk of their own abuses with a kind of childlike innocence. He never speaks for the facts, because he is a great enough artist to understand that facts must always speak for themselves. He is perhaps at his best when putting on the mask of an *ingénu* and talking with a most serious countenance about things which are taken seriously only by his characters and not by the reader. His irony consists in his pretending not to see any irony at all, although indirectly he makes us feel the wide gap between his own standpoint and that of his characters. The less he himself emphasizes this gap and pretends to be on the same level as his characters, the greater the comic-satirical atmosphere of the play. This atmosphere grows and grows ; but having reached its highest pitch, it suddenly bursts of itself and dissolves into the sinister last chord, whose effect is all the stronger because of the previous comicality. True, Gogol sometimes achieves his effects by various traditional " tricks " ; but in his case they are convincing because he knows how to motivate them psychologically. At the same time, the strictest artistic economy is preserved throughout, both in the construction and the details of the play. " In *The Revizor* there are no scenes to which the word ' better ' can be applied, because none of them is inferior to the rest," wrote Bielinsky ; " they are all excellent ; they are the necessary parts forming one artistic whole, which is rounded up not only by its external form, but also by its inner contents ; and so it is a self-sufficient world of its own."

When this comedy was finished an incredible thing happened : the censor passed it. This miracle was due, however, not to the censors, but to Czar Nicholas I. He read the manuscript of the comedy (brought to him by Zhukovsky) and at once ordered that *The Revizor* should be produced on the imperial stage. He himself was present at its first performance (March 19th, 1836), and laughing heartily, remarked : " Everyone has received his due and I most of all."

The play in itself is not a " realistic " copy of Russian provincial life, but an exaggerated picture of all those vices on which Gogol wished to vent his own indignation. It was his conscious craving for a higher form of life that severed him all the more from actual existence. It was his strong but unsatisfied need of reverence coupled with his utter incapacity to revere anything with genuine abandonment and passion that made him all the more aggressive. Hence he indulged at least in his *negative passion*—the passion of indictment, of anger, of laughter through tears. Having collected the necessary objective facts, he modified them according to his own inner need and constructed out of them a picture which he himself took for a mirror of real life. In fact, Gogol had to do so, because this was the only way in which he could attack and refute the reality he loathed. Once more he asserted himself against it—through his art.

The attack made by *The Revizor* was strong enough to raise everyone, and most of all, the corrupted officialdom, against Gogol. " The audiences felt the intensity of my anger even while laughing," he said later. But he could have added with equal truth that the production of this play had also been a notable social event : it was the first time that the so-called accusatory literature dared to speak in such terms from the Russian stage. The immediate result of this event was, however, far from being favourable to Gogol. The spectators enjoyed the piece, but they were cross with its author. For everyone saw himself personally insulted. Soon there was raised the hue and cry of the " patriots," who saw in him simply a slanderer of Holy Russia.

" All are against me," wrote Gogol to his

Moscow friend, the actor Schepkin, a few days after the first production of the play. " The old and respectable officials are shouting that since I dared to criticize the civil servants in this manner, there is nothing sacred ; the police, the merchants, the writers—all are against me."

Soon after this he jotted down his *Homegoing from the Theatre* (*Teatralny Razyezd*) in which he recorded very vividly some impressions of those onlookers who were for or against him.* At the same time Gogol made a few interesting remarks of his own, and eventually pointed out that there was at least one honest " character " in his piece—his laughter. He also emphasized the *ethical* significance of laughter.

In spite of all the attacks on Gogol, the piece continued to be played, and the theatre was always crowded. For even those who disliked it could not help enjoying it. But the more they laughed, the more angry they were with the man who was the originator of such double-faced laughter. Things went so far that Gogol soon became tired of the whole affair and decided to go abroad. " A contemporary author who writes comedies and describes manners must be as far from his own country as possible," he wrote to Pogodin before leaving Russia. " No prophet can earn glory in

* *Teatralny Razyezd* was, however, entirely finished only in 1842.

his own fatherland. I don't mind the fact that all classes of society have risen against me ; yet it is somewhat sad and depressing to see my own countrymen, whom I sincerely love, attack me with no justice, to see in what a perverted way they accept and interpret everything."

It was at the beginning of June, 1836, that Gogol left for Western Europe where he stayed until 1848, coming back to Russia only twice during that period.

V

Apart from the two comedies mentioned and the dramatic fragments, Gogol wrote a very vivid one-act piece, *The Gamblers*. It has only male parts and develops the old theme of a cheat who gets cheated by his own companions. In addition to his usual dramatic plasticity, Gogol shows here his gift for deliberate suspense and mystification : the finale of the plot is as unexpected for the onlooker as it is for the cheated cheat himself. This sketch was written some time between 1836 and 1840, and completed in 1842. Almost simultaneously with *The Revizor* Gogol conceived the plan (in 1835) of writing a tragedy from English History. But even a superficial insight into the specific qualities of Gogol's art is enough to convince one that writing tragedies was certainly not his proper vocation. Fortunately he did not go on with his plan. All that has remained of it are a few casual jottings under the title *Alfred*.

In order to clear up certain misunderstandings with regard to his *Revizor*, he published in its new edition of 1846 a kind of epilogue called *The Dénouement of the Revizor*. Owing to various influences which he had undergone abroad, Gogol made here an attempt at interpreting the whole piece in an allegorical way. The shabby town in which the gorodnichy ruled supreme he suddenly declared to be the town of our soul. Khlestakov was transmuted into a symbol of our volatile worldly conscience, and the Inspector-General himself into that of our true conscience which everyone will have to confront after death, etc. Such interpretation is of course ridiculous and entirely unconvincing. But if it obscures the piece, it shows certain new and disturbing features in Gogol himself. However, before dealing with this period of Gogol's life, we must say a few words about the importance of *The Revizor's* success for his personal destiny.

The strong effect produced by this play was bound to influence Gogol's further activities. Before that, he was not quite sure of his true vocation simply because he did not know in which direction he could assert his talents and ambitions to their utmost. In spite of all his triumphs, he seemed still to be groping and experimenting, as it were, with his own fate. [Together with literature he had tried also pedagogic activities (his professorship). His *Arabesque* shows how divided his interests were between literature proper and various quasi-scientific and pedagogic propensities. He planned a big History of Little Russia, and an even bigger History of the Middle Ages—" in eight or perhaps in nine volumes ". *The Revizor* however, put an end to it all. He saw what a great influence could be exercised by a writer who would tackle the realities of Russia and " describe manners ". This stimulated both his " realistic " and his ethical veins.] In short, he took leave of all romantic fancies and concentrated his efforts upon what he considered his true mission. Being sincerely convinced that he was a realist, he turned his eyes once more towards the actual Russia of that time. And the result of this effort was his longest and greatest work—*The Dead Souls.*

Chapter Six

The Dead Souls

I

LIKE most inwardly homeless people Gogol was fond of roaming and travelling. The distance, the vague infinity, attracted him with a magical force which became all the stronger the more dissatisfied he was with himself, with actual life and actual things. The swift *troika** running over the Russian plains appears in every chapter of his *Dead Souls*. And the narrative itself is sometimes interrupted by sudden dithyrambs in praise of the long, long road. " How strange, how alluring, stimulating and wonderful is the sound of the words ' on the road '. And how marvellous the road is ! The sunny day, the autumn leaves, the cold air . . . Wrapped more closely in one's winter coat, cap over ears, one huddles more snugly into the corner. For the last time a faint shiver passes through the limbs

* A chaise drawn by three horses.

and is followed by a pleasant warmth. The horses race along . . . how seductively drowsiness steals over one and the eyelids close and through sleep one hears, 'Not white were the snows', and the breathing of the horses and the rumble of the wheels. . . . My God, how glorious is at times the long, long road! How often have I, drowning and perishing, clutched at thee, and always thou hast rescued and preserved me!"

So it is hardly surprising that Gogol spent most of his time after 1836 in wandering over Europe. From Petersburg he first went to Vevey, then to Paris. In March, 1837, he settled down in Rome, but in the summer of the same year he went to Baden-Baden, where he met his friend, Mme. Rosset-Smirnova. He then returned to Rome for a longer period, but in September, 1839, he was in Petersburg again, then in Moscow. The summer of 1840 he spent in Vienna, the autumn and the winter in Rome which he left in 1841 for Germany and for Russia. In May, 1842, he suddenly re-appeared in Petersburg, whence he went to Austria; from Austria to Munich, from Munich to Rome, from Rome to Florence, from Florence to Germany, and from Germany back to Rome. In January 1845, he was in Paris (with the Vielgorsky family), a year later in Germany. At the beginning of 1848 he went to Palestine, but towards the end of May he was back in Russia. There he stopped for a while in the Ukraine, but he soon left for Moscow. Yet he did not settle down there either, but continued to wander : now he was in Kaluga, then in the Ukraine, or in Odessa. At last he came again to Moscow, where he died.

This is only a small number of the places and countries he had visited, especially in the years of his voluntary exile from Russia. There was, however, one place he loved above all other spots on earth, and where he stayed and worked most. This was Rome. No sooner had he reached Italy than the southerner in him awoke. He began to feel at home in this world, and when he saw Rome he fell in love with it at once. The spirit of the Middle Ages, still lingering over the papal city, its picturesque character, its mystery and seclusion, the solemn theatrical ritual of the Catholic liturgy, the distance from " modern " ideas—all this appealed to Gogol's romantic estheticism. It was the atmosphere of delightful unreality that entranced him, as it were, in the almost mediaeval papal Rome. And this was natural. For Gogol had never liked nor understood any other epoch but the Middle Ages. He was an absolute stranger in the Europe of his time—in that Europe which was fermenting with new ideas and ideals ; which was entirely engrossed in its political and social struggles. He ignored it; he probably did not even wish to understand it. Besides, Gogol's education was at that time hardly solid enough to make him take a broader interest in Europe and in Western culture. He did not care for European literature either. His friend, P. V. Annichkov, says (in his *Gogol in Rome*) that the Gogol of that period "had not read anything of French *belles-lettres*, and began to read Molière only after a severe upbraiding on the part of Pushkin for having neglected such an author. He knew Shakespeare equally badly, while Goethe and German literature simply did not exist for him. Of all foreign writers there was only one name he knew not by hearsay and by rumour only—the name of Walter Scott." With all this, Gogol found his new abode so congenial that the conservative Rome and Italy played an important part in his life. "With what relief I gave up Switzerland and flew to my sweetheart, to my beauty—Italy," he wrote from there. "She is mine! No one will take her away from me. This is my real birth-place. Russia, Petersburg, snows, scoundrels, departments, University-chair, theatre—all this was only a dream. Now I have awakened in my true homeland. The powerful hand of Providence has cast me under Italy's glittering sky, with a special aim as it were—that I should forget all about my grief, about people, about everything, and that I should cling to her gorgeous beauty. She has now replaced all for me."

In Rome he even regained a certain amount of joy and expansiveness. There he breathed the real romance ; so he could neglect for a time the imaginary one. And so from his " lovely far-away paradise " he now threw a glance at his own country, and treated it with the same *arrière-pensée* as in *The Revizor*, but on a grander scale. This he did in his immortal *Dead Souls.*

II

The opening chapters of this work must have been written already in 1835, as we see from a letter of Gogol to Pushkin (Oct. 1835). The very idea of it had been taken by him from Pushkin—perhaps even against Pushkin's own will, for he himself had a vague intention of writing a realistic prose-work on the same motive as *The Dead Souls.* It is quite possible that Gogol hastened to make use of the subject mentioned by his friend ; but even if this conjecture be true, Pushkin was the first to become enthusiastic about Gogol's draft. While listening to Gogol's reading he laughed heartily. But soon his face became gloomy and he could not suppress the exclamation, " Lord, what a sad country our Russia is."

Gogol probably intended at first to write a kind of humorous and satirical work on a bigger scale than his former stories. But partly under the strong effect produced by his *Revizor* and partly during the process of elaboration, his original conception widened. " I am working again at my *Dead Souls* which I had begun at Petersburg," he announced to Zhukovsky from Paris (Dec. 1836) " I have remade all that was done before, I have reconsidered the whole plan, and now am working it out quietly as if I were writing a chronicle . . . If I ever complete this work in the manner I should like to—what a colossal, what an original subject! What a varied crowd! The whole of Russia will appear in it! This is going to be the first production of mine that will preserve my name."

The construction of this novel, or epic—as Gogol himself calls it, reminds one of *Don Quixote* or of *The Pickwick Papers*: its development is based on the travels and encounters made by its main hero, Chichikov. Later on, Gogol conceived the idea of enlarging the epic into a trilogy, in the manner of Dante's *Divina Comedia*; but he finished its first part only—the part which represents a kind of Inferno of the actual Russia.

For here Gogol did the same as in his *Revizor:* he collected in one piece all that was bad in his own country and condensed it with all the intensity of true art into a tremendous picture which, though realistic in its single elements, represents a distorted subjective vision of life as a whole.

Like most Russian masterpieces, *The Dead Souls* is simple in its conception. It has no love-story proper, no intricate and "clever" plot. It is just a series of *genre* pictures, of types painted with an incredible skill and plastic sense.

"A rather pretty little chaise on springs, such as bachelors, half-pay officers, staff-captains, landowners with about a hundred serfs—in short, all such as are spoken of as 'gentlemen of the middling sort'—drive about in, rolled in at the gates of the hotel of the provoncial town of N—. In the chaise sat a gentleman, not handsome but not bad looking, not too stout and not too thin; it could not be said that he was old, neither could he be described as extremely young. His arrival in the town created no sensation whatever and was not accompanied by anything remarkable. Only two Russian peasants standing at the door of the tavern facing the hotel made some observations, with reference, however, to the carriage rather than to its occupant, 'My eye', said one to the other, 'isn't that a wheel!

What do you think ? Would that wheel, if so it chanced, get to Moscow or would it never get there ?' 'It would,' answered the other. 'But to Kazan now, I don't think it would get there ?' 'It wouldn't get to Kazan,' answered the other. With this the conversation ended. Moreover, just as the chaise drove up to the hotel it was met by a young man in extremely short and narrow white canvas trousers, in a coat with fashionable cut-away tails and a shirt-front fastened with a Tula breastpin adorned with a bronze pistol. The young man turned round, stared at the chaise, holding his cap which was almost flying off in the wind, and went on his way."

This is how the epic begins. And, contrary to Gogol's former works, it develops in a slow and quiet narrative tempo ; bit by bit is added, until we begin to follow with growing eagerness every trifle, and become absorbed by the atmosphere of the whole. We follow Pavel Ivanovitch Chichikov—for this is the full name of the hero—to his room in the hotel, we see him eating, dressing, conversing with the waiter, then driving out to call on the local potentates. There is nothing striking about him, except perhaps his great adaptability and his artful politeness. Especially in conversation with the ruling personages he always knows how to put in the right word. "To the governor he hinted, as it were casually, that one travelled in his province as in Paradise, that the roads were everywhere like velvet and that governments which appointed wise rulers were worthy of the greatest praise. To the police-master he said something very flattering about the town-police ; while in conversation with the deputy-governor and the president of the court who were still only civil councillors, he twice said by mistake 'your Excellency ', which greatly gratified them." We learn further that he avoids talking about his own person, but when he feels he must say something about himself, never goes beyond a few commonplace and discreet remarks that he had suffered from his enemies for the sake of Right and that he would like to settle down in peace in some quiet little place or other. Then again we witness his careful preparations for the evening party at the governor's. "After a brief nap he asked for soap and water and spent an extremely long time scrubbing his cheeks with soap, putting his tongue into them to make them stand out ; then, taking a towel off the shoulders of the waiter, wiped his face in all directions, beginning from behind his ears, first giving two snorts right in the face of the waiter ; then he put on his shirt-front before the looking-glass, tweaked out two hairs that were protuding from his nose, and immediately after that attired himself in a short cranberry-coloured dress-coat. Having thus arrayed himself he drove in his own carriage through the immensely wide streets, illuminated by the faint light that came from the windows glimmering here and there."

At the governor's he charms everyone by his manners, his tact, his gentlemanly exterior. He soon manages to make acquaintance with the local landowners, such as the ultra-polished and sugary Manilov, the clumsy country-bear Sobakievitch, and others, but always tactfully—without intruding upon any one. In short, " the newcomer was quite at ease on every occasion and showed himself an experienced man of the world. Whatever the subject of conversation he could always keep it up : were horse-breeding discussed, he talked about horse-breeding : if they conversed about the best dogs, on that subject too he made very apt observations ; if they touched on a case inquired into by the court of justice, he showed that he was not ignorant of court procedure ; if the topic were a game of billiards, he was not at sea in billiards either ; if the conversation turned upon virtue, he made excellent reflections upon virtue and even with tears in his eyes ; upon the preparation of hot punch, he was an authority on punch, too ; upon overseers of customs and excise officers, he discoursed about them as though he had been himself an excise officer or overseer of the customs. But it was noteworthy that he succeeded in accompanying all this with a certain sedateness, and knew very well how to behave. He spoke neither too loud nor too low, but exactly as he ought. Take him how you would, he was a thoroughly gentlemanly man. All the government officials were pleased at the arrival of the newcomer. The governor pronounced that he was a man thoroughly to be depended upon : the public prosecutor said that he was a practical man ; the colonel of the gendarmes said that he was a well-informed and estimable man ; the police-master that he was an estimable and agreeable man ; the police-master's wife that he was a most agreeable and most amiable man. Though Sobakievitch rarely said anything good of anyone, yet even he, after returning rather late from town, undressing and getting into bed beside his scraggy wife, said to her : ' I spent the evening at the governor's, my love, and dined at the police-master's and made the acquaintance of a collegiate councillor called Pavel Ivanovitch Chichikov, a very agreeable man ! ' To which his spouse responded with : ' Hm ! ' and kicked him."

III

Having thus introduced to us the hero and his

new surroundings, Gogol proceeds to unveil in the subsequent chapters, step by step, the strange object of Chichikov's errands. To put it briefly, this paragon of gentlemanliness and social charm has embarked upon a delicate undertaking: with his troika and his two servants, Petrushka and Selifan, he travels from one landowner to the other with the object of buying those dead serfs (or "souls" as the serfs were called in Russia) whose deaths have not yet been registered. As the census of serfs took place once in ten years only, Chichikov devised a clever plan by which to enrich himself. Knowing that till the next census there would be no official control of serfs, he decided to buy as many fictitious "souls" as possible and pawn them in the Bank as the living ones. "Suppose I buy all who are dead," he calculates, "before the new census lists are sent out, if I get, let us say, a thousand of them, and suppose the Trustee Committee gives me two hundred roubles a soul: why, there's a fortune of two hundred thousand! And now is a good time, there has just been an epidemic, the peasants have died, thank goodness, in great numbers."*

* Gogol made, however—unwittingly—some serious mistakes about legal transactions. Already S. Aksakov had pointed out to him in a letter (July 3rd, 1842) that serfs, for the purpose of being transferred elsewhere, could be sold only together with their families, whereas Chichikov refused to buy women. There are also a few other points which prove that Gogol was not well acquainted with Russian laws on this matter.

This is the actual object of Chichikov's wanderings. As the book is constructed upon the principle of a travel novel, its author has the chance of displaying all his gifts. He lets his hero meet all sorts of people and most of them provide excellent material for such a portrait-painter as Gogol. Take the sentimental fool, Manilov ;* the shrewd animal, Sobakievitch ; or Korobochka, an almost half-witted old woman and yet an extremely sharp manageress of her own affairs ; the " broad-natured " cheat, scandal-monger and eternal *ami-cochon*, Nozdryov ; or the miser, Plyushkin, whose personality had been shrunk but to one single vice, feeding on him until it reduced him to a mere tatter of humanity. Then the whole of the provincial society with its balls, whist-drives, intrigues, gossip—with all its empty and senseless existence.

As to single characters, Gogol paints them here rather than " impersonates ". Yet he makes each of them live an intensified life, both as an individual and as a type, that is, as a symbolic representative of a whole category of human beings. His figures are symbolic owing to their very condensed " realism." Chichikov himself is a symbol in so far as he typifies the respectable and grabbing mediocrity : the modern

* According to Kallash, there are embodied in Manilov certain features of Gogol's own father.

speculator, or the rising bourgeois *in excelsis*, whose dreams do not go beyond wealth for its own sake, beyond a buxom wife and a host of descendants. Khlestakov looks almost an innocent baby by the side of this weighty and respectable gentleman who collects the " dead souls " all over Russia without suspecting that his own soul is utterly and hopelessly dead. Chichikov's background, too, is equally symbolic. Through all the grotesque trifles and trivialities there looms the great tedium and the drab monotony of our life as a whole. Behind Gogol's grinning laughter we feel the great boredom and the vulgarity of an age in which the very soul of mankind seems to be dying a slow and imperceptible death. " Those who have dissected my literary abilities, were not able to find out the essential characteristics of my nature," says Gogol elsewhere. " Only Pushkin was able to do it. He always asserted that no author except myself has such a capacity for bringing out all the trivialities of life, of describing so well the vulgarity of the mediocre man, or of opening one's eyes on those small things which generally remain unobserved."

Gogol's *Dead Souls* represents the highest pitch of this capacity. One becomes in fact so absorbed by various significant trifles of his work that one often forgets all about the plot itself.

Yet the trees do not conceal the forest. Gogol puts one trivial bit beside the other in order to produce a kind of enormous mosaic which gradually forms itself into a terrifying picture of human life. This is perhaps one of the reasons why one never tires of his quiet detailed descriptions, and least of all when they refer to some character or other. We absorb them with a growing interest until his grotesque figures stand before us more alive than in reality, alive to such a degree that they almost persecute our imagination. Take for example this description of the landowner, Sobakievitch :

" When Chichikov stole a sidelong glance at Sobakievitch he struck him on this occasion as being extremely like a middle-sized bear. To complete the resemblance, his dresscoat was precisely the colour of bear's skin, his sleeves were long, his trousers were long, he ambled from side to side as he walked and was continually treading on other people's feet. His face was burnt as dark red as a copper penny. We all know that there are a great many faces in the world over the carving of which nature has spent no great pains, has used no delicate tools such as files or gimlets, but has simply rough-hewn them with a swing of the arm : one stroke of the axe and there's a nose, another and there are the lips, the eyes are bored with a great drill, and without polishing it off, nature thrusts it into the world, saying, 'This will do'. Just such an uncouth and strangely hewn countenance was that of Sobakievitch : he held it rather drooping than erect, he did not turn his neck at all, and in consequence of this immobility he rarely looked at the person to whom he was speaking but always stared away at the corner of the stove or at the door. Chichikov stole another glance at him as they reached the dining room ; he was a bear, a regular bear ; to complete the strange resemblance his name was actually Mihail Semyonovitch.* Knowing his habit of treading on people's feet, Chichikov moved his own feet very cautiously and made way for him to go first. Apparently Sobakievitch was aware of this failing and at once asked whether he had caused him any inconvenience, but Chichikov thanked him and said that he had so far suffered no discomfort."

Together with this, Gogol devised in his *Dead Souls* an excellent means of showing at one stroke the inner essence of the main types concerned, simply by their reaction to Chichikov's delicate proposal. The latter also gives us an opportunity of studying Chichikov himself every time from a new angle. For his illegal errand is of such a sort that it requires continuous and

* The pet name given to bears by the Russian peasants is Misha, or Mishka, which is a diminutive of Mihail.

extreme caution, as well as subtlety, in probing the ground and finding out whether it would be safe to broach the subject at all, and whether there are any chances of success. So each new meeting on his part becomes a new psychological task which has to be solved by itself. Such a solution forms at the same time the climax of each separate chapter. Since we have just left Chichikov in Sobakievich's company, we may listen perhaps to the beginning of their conversation about the delicate matter.

" Sobakievitch bent his head slightly, and prepared to hear what the business might be. Chichikov approached the subject indirectly, touched on the Russian empire in general, and spoke with great appreciation of its vast extent, said that even the ancient Roman empire was not so vast . . . (Sobakievitch still listened with his head bowed) and that in accordance with the existing ordinances of the government, whose fame had no equal, souls on the census list who had ended their earthly career, were, until the next census was taken, reckoned as though they were alive, in order to avoid burdening the government departments with a multitude of petty and unimportant details and increasing the complexity of the administrative machinery, complicated as it is . . . (Sobakievitch still listened with his head bowed) and that justifiable as this arrangement was, it yet put a somewhat heavy burden on many landowners, compelling them to pay the tax as though for living serfs, and that through a sentiment of personal respect for him, he was prepared to some extent to relieve him of this burdensome obligation. In regard to the real subject of his remarks, Chichikov expressed himself very cautiously and never spoke of the souls as dead, but invariably as non-existent. Sobakievitch still listened as before with his head bent, and not a trace of anything approaching expression showed on his face. It seemed as though in that body there was no soul at all, or if there were that it was not in its proper place, but, as with the immortal Boney, somewhere far away and covered with so thick a shell that whatever was stirring at the bottom of it produced not the faintest ripple on the surface.

" 'And so . . . ?' said Chichikov, waiting, not without some perturbation, for an answer.

" 'You want the dead souls ?' inquired Sobakievitch very simply, with no sign of surprise, as though they had been talking of corn.

" 'Yes,' said Chichikov, and again he softened the expression, adding, 'non-existent ones'.

" 'There are some ; to be sure there are,' said Sobakievitch.

" 'Well, if you have any, you will doubtless be glad to get rid of them ?'

" 'Certainly, I am willing to sell them,' said Sobakievitch, slightly raising his head and reflecting that doubtless the purchaser would make some profit out of them.

" 'Deuce take it!' thought Chichikov to himself. 'He is ready to sell them before I drop hint of it!' And aloud he said 'And at what price, for instance? Though, indeed it is a queer sort of goods . . . it seems odd to speak of the price.' "

And so on. One could quote several other passages. Chichikov's conversation with Korobochka, with the irresponsible Nozdryov who nearly beat him in a fit of haggling fever, or with Plyushkin; but it is difficult to decide which chapter is the best. They are all supreme. At the same time, each character speaks a language of his own which is as typical of him as are the features of his face. Although each chapter has a climax and can be read almost independently of the others, it converges towards the climax of the book in such a way as to make Chichikov's downfall almost as sudden and unexpected as the downfall of the gorodnichy in *The Revizor*. For this is what happened: Chichikov returned with his fictitious "souls" to the town. There the rumour spread that he was a millionaire buying the serfs for cash and with the express object of settling them on his recently bought estate somewhere in the far south—in the Kherson district, as he himself had vaguely hinted. The whole town was now excited over it. The affable millionarie Chichikov became the hero of the day. In lionizing him the people seemed to forget the limits of hospitality and kindness. And the ladies of course found him irresistible. One day he even received a pathetic letter from an entirely unknown damsel, a letter which began with the resolute, "Yes, I must write to you!" and finished with these touching and heart-felt lines :

> " Two turtle doves will show thee
> Where my cold ashes lie,
> And sadly murmuring tell thee
> How in tears I did die."

How many more charms and perfections they must have discovered in him on hearing fantastic accounts of his millions, of his estates, and particularly of his being a bachelor! Knowing that he would come to the governor's ball they exhausted all their wits, their energies, and their husbands' purses to outstrip each other in toilettes. The prospect of Chichikov's presence was no joking matter! His appearance made in fact an extraordinary impression, not only on the fair sex, but on all without exception. " Everyone turned to greet him, one with cards in his hands, another at the most interesting point in the conversation as he uttered the words : 'And the lower district court maintains in answer that . . .' but what the district court did maintain he abandoned altogether and hastened to welcome our hero. 'Pavel Ivanovitch ! Ah, goodness me, Pavel Ivanovitch ! Dear Pavel Ivanovitch ! Honoured Pavel Ivanovitch ! My dear soul, Pavel Ivanovitch ! Oh here you are, Pavel Ivanovitch ! Here he is, our Pavel Ivanovitch ! Allow me to embrace you, Pavel Ivanovitch ! Hand him over, let me give him a good kiss, my precious Pavel Ivanovitch ! Chichikov instantly felt himself clasped in the embrace of several friends. He had hardly succeeded in completely extricating himself from the embrace of the president, when he found himself in the arms of the police-master ; the police-master passed him on to the inspector of the medical board ; the inspector of the medical board handed him over to the government contractor, and the latter passed him on to the architect. . . . The governor, who was at the moment standing by some ladies with a motto from a bonbon in one hand and a lap-dog in the other, dropped both motto and lap-dog on the floor on seeing him, the dog raised a shrill yelp—in short, Chichikov was the centre of extraordinary joy and delight."

But at the very height of his social success, something unexpected happened. It must be said that, in spite of all his caution, Chichikov had made one serious slip during his pourparlers : thinking that the incorrigible spendthrift, Nozdryov, might be inclined to sell some of his dead " souls ", he had confided the object of his errand to him also. Nozdryov, who felt as uncomfortable without gossip and scandal as a fish feels without water, soon made the best of it. True, he was practically never sober, but for this very reason neither his temperament nor his feverish imagination knew any restraint whatever. As luck would have it, Nozdryov, too, suddenly appeared at the governor's ball. And what was worse, he came in high spirits. At the very moment when the governor asked our " precious Pavel Ivanovitch " to arbitrate between him and two ladies as to whether women's love were constant or not, Nozdryov ran straight to him.

" Ah, the Kherson landowner, the Kherson landowner ! " he shouted, as he came up, and went off into a guffaw so that his cheeks, fresh and red as a spring rose, shook with laughter. " Well ? have you bought a lot of dead souls ? I expect you don't know, your Excellency," he bawled addressing the governor, " he deals in dead souls ! Upon my word ! I say, Chichikov ! Let me tell you, I may say it as a friend, we are all your friends here, and here is his Excellency too—I'd hang you, upon my soul, I would . . ."

This unpleasant incident was the beginning of Chichikov's downfall, which was hastened too, by other circumstances. So during that very night, while the sleepless " Kherson landowner " was cursing Nozdryov and all his ancestors, a strange equipage was heard rumbling and creaking through the deserted streets of the town—" it was not like a coach, nor a carriage, nor a chaise, but it was more like a full-cheeked rounded melon on wheels. The cheeks of this melon, that is the door, which bore traces of yellow paint, shut very badly owing to the rickety condition of the handles and locks, which were tied up with string. The melon was full of cotton cushions in the shape of pouches, rolling pins, and simple pillows, stuffed with sacks of bread, fancy loaves, doughnuts and pasties, and bread rings made of boiled dough. Chicken pies and salt-fish pies peeped out at the top." In this creaking melon on wheels sat the silly and stingy Korobochka who hurried to the town to make enquiries about the latest price of the dead " souls ", for she was frightened out of her wits by the sheer idea that Chichikov might have cheated her.

IV

Suspicion once aroused ran its complete course. It soon gave way to the wildest conjectures, hints and slander. And the most active element in this storm rising so ominously against Chichikov was again the prattling ladies of the town. Some of them were against him chiefly because they thought themselves slighted by Chichikov, who at the ball had paid too much attention to the governor's pretty daughter ; others because they had praised him too much before ; others again—but who can tell all the reasons of a woman's offence ? With an imagination at least as prolific as that of Nozdryov, they invented all sorts of absurd things about their former hero ; and, what is so natural with women, they were the first to believe their own inventions.

" Only imagine, he makes his appearance armed to the teeth like some Rinaldo Rinaldini and demands : ' Sell me all your souls that are dead '. Korobochka answers him very reasonably, saying : ' I can't sell them because they are dead.' ' No ', he said ' they are not dead, they are mine, it's my business to know whether they are dead or not,' says he. ' They are not dead, not dead,' he shouts, ' not dead ! ' In fact he makes a fearful scene ; all the village rushes up, the children cry, everybody is shouting, no one can make out what's the matter, it was simply an *horreur*, *horreur*, *horreur* . . . ."

The whole population was in a stir. Even those who had not been lured out of their beds or from their divans for years and years, now joined in the general gossip. Some worthy ladies spread the rumour that Chichikov wanted to elope with the governor's daughter, and that together with Nozdryov he had already made all the necessary arrangements. This rumour was soon replaced by the detailed account that Chichikov had begun by courting the girl's mother and only after a prolonged liaison with her asked for the hand of her daughter ; but as the mother found such a combination too impious, she refused ; so the desolate Chichikov decided to elope. . . . They invented many other things. In a word, while Chichikov was confined to bed for a few days, owing to a cold, " society " rose against him with the same stupid, nonsensical spontaneity with which it had welcomed him on his arrival. The most incredible lies about his career were afloat. At last no one could make head or tail of them. The figure of Chichikov became a disturbing mystery, it seemed to hover like a ghost over the town and haunt it by its very vagueness. His acquaintances were actually frightened beyond measure. Who was he in fact ? Some thought he was a maker of counterfeit notes ; others that he was a disguised brigand and robber chief ; others again that he might perhaps even be Napoleon himself, wandering under a false name over Holy Russia in order to ruin her.

Agitation and fear increased with the vagueness of the rumours. The people who were particularly excited and perturbed were the officials. One of them, the thick-browed prosecutor, was so affected by all these mysterious stories that he "fell to brooding, and suddenly, for no rhyme or reason, as the saying is, died. Whether it was a paralytic stroke or some other attack, anyway, while he was sitting at the table he flopped forward on his face. As is usual on such occasions, people cried out, 'Good God!' and flinging up their hands, sent for the doctor to bleed him, but saw that the prosecutor was a soulless corpse. It was only then they recognized with regret that he really had a soul, though he had always been too modest to show it."

Chichikov was during all that time lying in his bed—with a bag filled with camomile and camphor on his swollen cheeks—and had no idea of what was going on in the town. So on his recovery he set off (dressed spick and span, sprinkled with eau-de-cologne and warmly wrapped up) to pay his visits. But to his great surprise, he either was not let in at all or was received with undisguised dismay and even horror. The only person who was not in the least afraid of his company was Nozdryov, who suddenly called on him at the hotel, as if nothing had happened. It was he who reported to

Chichikov, with great relish, all the scandalous talk afloat and finished by asking the " Kherson landowner " to lend him three thousand roubles.

Seeing how bad things were, Chichikov left the town the very next day. His carriage was held up for a few minutes by the funeral procession of the prosecutor. While looking from behind the curtain of his chaise at the coffin, at the bareheaded officials, and at the mourning caps of the ladies, Chichikov fell to musing in his own characteristic fashion. " So much for the prosecutor ! He lived and lived and then he died ! And now they will print in the newspapers that he passed away to the grief of his subordinates and of all humanity, an honoured citizen, a devoted father, a faithful husband, and they will write all sorts of nonsense ; they will very likely add that he was followed to the grave by the lamentations of widows and orphans ; and yet if one goes into the facts of the case, it turns out on investigation that there was nothing special about you but your thick eyebrows. . . . Well, it is a good thing we met the funeral, they say meeting a funeral means happiness."

Chichikov's departure, and the history of his former career, with all its cunning and well-mannered scoundrelism, its " brilliance " and consecutive mishaps, conclude the first book of *The Dead Souls*.

THE DEAD SOULS

V

As to the rest of the epic, only five uncompleted chapters of the second part have been saved. There is a difference in opinions with regard to the date of these chapters. According to V. Kallash's investigations, they belong not to the first version which was burnt in 1845, but to that written afterwards. This fragmentary second part shows on the whole a more dynamic action, perhaps a greater objectivity, and also a somewhat higher moral plane of its characters. Chichikov himself gets trapped by his own trickery and is released from prison owing to the philanthropic merchant Murazov, who puts him on the track of virtue. He seems to find this new course somewhat unfamiliar ; yet after all his troubles we see him driving away with a vague promise of real change. "The inner state of his soul might be compared with a building that has been pulled down to be rebuilt into a new one, and the new one has not yet been begun, because no definite plan has come from the architect, and the workmen are left in suspense."

It was in the second part that Gogol tried to reveal to us the Purgatory of the Russian soul with a note of purification, in order to fulfil later on that promise which he had already given his readers in the first part (Chapter VII.) : "Perhaps in this very novel some chords hitherto unstruck may be discerned, the infinite wealth of the Russian soul may be set forth, a man endowed with divine qualities, or a wonderful Russian maiden, such as cannot be found elsewhere in the world, with the marvellous beauty of a woman's soul made up of generous impulse and sacrifice, may emerge. And all the virtuous people of other races will seem dead beside them, as a book is dead beside the living word."

He gave us in fact a few positive characters : the ideal landowner Kostanzhoglo (Skudrozhoglo); the ideal merchant Murazov ; the ideal Russian girl Ulinka ; even an ideal governor. But unfortunately, none of these types is convincing : they are simply walking puppets, pasted with rhetorical and moralizing labels. At the same time, all his negative figures are well sketched out, whether the indolent Tentetnikov, the half-mad Koshkaryov, the sloppy Hlobuyev, or the swilling gourmand Pyetuh. But even if taken together with its fragmentary second part, which was published only after Gogol's death, *The Dead Souls* is one of the imperishable masterpieces of European literature. It is the highest achievement of Gogol's genius.

The "official" critics of those days—Senkovsky, Bulgarin, Gretch and even Polevoy—

hardly found words enough with which to abuse this work, as well as its author, whom they compared with Paul de Kock. Before that Gogol had considerable trouble also with the censors, one ofwhom had shouted on hearing the title of the book : " Dead Souls—no, I'll never allow such a thing ; our soul is immortal ; there is no dead soul ; the author rises against immortality." Nevertheless the work found at once its due appreciation among those men whose taste and judgment did matter. Bielinsky was enthusiastic about it. And the young Aksakov went so far as to liken Gogol to Homer and Shakespeare. Since then the great merits of the book have been recognized all over the world. And what is more important, even now—more than eighty years after its publication—it has not lost the bloom of its freshness. Like all great art, it remains eternally modern.

Although *The Dead Souls* is still remotely connected with the didactic-satirical novels which were represented in Russia chiefly by Naryezhny and Bulgarin, it is a new departure in many respects. Yet no works are free of faults ; even Gogol's great epic is not an exception. Its construction is not entirely compact : the chapters, instead of growing out of each other, are put one beside the other ; and to the end of the epic we are not quite sure as to where is the real central knot of the whole work. The intensity of its finale is weakened by the account of Chichikov's former career at the end of the novel and not before. Then Chichikov himself vanishes at last in a kind of vague distance ; Gogol shows us neither his inevitable catastrophe nor the inevitable perspective of his further fate. The idea of his regeneration apparently entered Gogol's head during his "mystical" period. It is, however, doubtful whether Gogol could have depicted convincingly such an inner transition in his main hero. For Gogol's characters never *develop* ; they exist but as finished portraits painted by an artist who is powerful only when dealing with fixed and static inner life. One could also point out that Gogol's rôle of guide and interpreter in the epic itself is not always successful : the lyrical and the moralizing passages, many of which he interpolated probably after the work had been already finished, do not always harmonize with the general tone of the book. On the other hand, they often provide a clue to Gogol himself. For with all its surface objectivity, *The Dead Souls* is Gogol's most subjective production. Hence its frequent contradictions—as if it had been written by two different men. The very end of the first part confirms this, for, after the gloomiest pictures of Russia and the Russians, Gogol suddenly passes to ecstatic rapture over his country as if wishing to drown, in his lyrical intoxication, his own sadness. Here is the famous passage with which we will also conclude this chapter :

" Chichikov merely smiled as he lightly swayed on his leather cushion, for he loved rapid driving. And what Russian does not love rapid driving ? How should his soul, that craves to be lost in a whirl, to carouse without stint, to say at times 'Damnation take it all ! '—how should his soul not love it ? How not love it when there is a feeling in it of something ecstatic and marvellous ? One fancies that an unseen force has caught one up on its wing and one flies oneself, and everything flies too : milestones fly by, merchants on the front seats of their tilt-carts fly to meet one, the forest flies by on both sides with dark rows of firs and pines, with the ring of the axe and the caw of crows : the whole road flies into the unknown, retreating distance ; and there is something terrible in this rapid flitting by, in which there is no time to distinguish the vanishing objects, and only the sky over one's head and the light clouds and the moon that struggles through them seem motionless. Ah, troika, bird of a troika ! Who was it first thought of thee ? Sure, thou could'st only have been born among a spirited people—in that land that does not care to do things by halves, but has spread, a vast plain, over half the world, and one may count its milestones, till one's eyes are dizzy ! And there is nothing elaborate, one would think, about thy construction ; it is not held together by iron screws—no, a deft Yaroslav peasant fitted thee up and put thee together, hastily, roughly, with nothing but axe and drill. The driver wears no German top boots : he has a beard and gauntlets and sits upon goodness knows what, but when he stands up and swings his whip and strikes up a song—the horses fly like a whirlwind, the spokes of the wheels are blended into one revolving disc, the road quivers, and the pedestrian cries out, halting in alarm—and the troika dashes away and away ! . . . And already all that can be seen in the distance is something flinging up the dust and whirling through the air.

" And, Russia, art not thou too flying onwards like a spirited troika that nothing can overtake ? The road is smoking under thee, the bridges rumble, everything falls back and is left behind ! The spectator stands still, struck dumb by the divine miracle : is it not a flash of lightning from heaven ? What is the meaning of this terrifying onrush ? What mysterious force is hidden in this troika, never seen before ? Ah, horses, horses—what horses ! Is the whirlwind hidden under your manes ? Is there some delicate sense tingling in every vein ? They hear the familiar song over their heads—at once in unison they strain their iron chests and scarcely touching the earth with their hoofs are transformed almost into straight lines flying through the air—and the troika rushes on, full of divine inspiration. . . . Russia, whither flyest thou? Answer! She gives no answer. The ringing of the bells melts into music; the air, torn to shreds, whirs and rushes like the wind, everything there is on earth is flying by and the other states and nations, with looks askance, make way for her and draw aside."

Chapter Seven

ART AND ETHICS

I

Gogol made several references to the chaotic nature of his own personality. But had he not revealed this truth about himself, his writings would be quite sufficient to do so; for they are—in Gogol's own words—but a disguised history of his own soul. True, he wrote his *Evenings* chiefly in order to look away from himself; yet even there the themes and symbols have a subconscious relation to Gogol's inner life. After his *Mirgorod*, however, he created both his " humorous " and his " realistic " works, through looking into himself only. So nothing is more personal than the apparent realism and the laughter of Gogol.

" None of my readers knows that in laughing at my characters they laughed at myself," he confessed in 1847. " In me there was a collection of all possible defects and in a greater quantity than in any other man. . . . If they had suddenly and all together appeared before my eyes I would have hanged myself . . . I began to depict in my heroes my own nastiness. This is how I did it. Having taken some bad feature of mine or other, I persecuted it under a different name and in a different rôle, endeavouring to make it appear before my eyes as my deadly enemy—an enemy who had inflicted a terrible injury upon me ; I persecuted it with malice, with irony, with anything I could get hold of. Had anyone seen those monsters which came from under my pen at the beginning, he would have shivered with fear."

This passage gives us a reliable clue to that Gogol who was dissatisfied with the world because he was dissatisfied with himself. His misanthropy had its root in his moral introspection. For in his fight for a higher realization of life he was always morbidly conscious of his own faults, which he magnified and then pursued with ruthless cruelty. This is why his negative types are intensely convincing. His art, which at first had been stimulated by his need of a romantic shelter, gradually expanded into that struggle with reality and with himself which found its most perfect expression in *The Dead Souls*. Such a creative process naturally made him concentrate all his energy on those aspects of life which were most likely to foster his own inner discharge, his *catharsis*. The plot as such became of secondary importance. What mattered to him were the characters and those tedious features of our existence on which he could avenge both his own defects and his outraged idealism.

This alone may account for the fact that Gogol was incapable—one is tempted to say organically incapable—of creating positive characters. Whenever he tried to shape them he usually lost his *élan* and his intensity of vision. At the utmost he could reason them out after a mechanical pattern. On the other hand, in so far as Gogol's " realism " was due to his inner need of ridiculing his own defects, his ultimate impulse towards creation was in essence an ethical one. At the bottom of his greatest artistic achievements one can discover hidden moral roots which he duly disguised when transferring them to the esthetic plane. It was the hidden romantic moralist who in some way or other had to give the last sanction to Gogol's esthetic activities. Eventually art became for him a means to a higher form of life, a path towards his own self-realization.

It was on this path, however, that Gogol soon encountered two great obstacles. The first of them was the usual tendency of all moral impulses to emancipate themselves from art and become rationalistic ; that is, to degenerate simply into moralizing preaching. And the second obstacle was Gogol's own "inferiority complex", which always fostered his egotism, conceit and worldly ambitions—all those features which often made him so unpleasant, so self-assertive, that even his best friends could not help being repelled by him. Pletnyov, for instance, scolded him frankly in a letter: "Well, who are you? As a man you are a secretive, self-loving and conceited creature, ready to sacrifice everything for the sake of glory. And what are you like as a friend? But do friends exist for you at all?" Sergius Aksakov himself says that in Gogol "there was something repellent . . . I don't know whether anyone ever loved Gogol the man. I think not; it would indeed be impossible."

II

It is here that we touch upon the very core of Gogol's inner dilemma, which consisted in the continuous divergence between two impulses he could never reconcile: the urge towards a higher self-realization and that towards egotistic self-assertion. Both were on different planes. Hence in the ethical respect also we often have to deal with two Gogols who diverge to such an extent as to exclude one another. While the first Gogol always shows a sincere and passionate desire to transcend his own *Ego* in the name of higher values, his self-assertive double always drags him back, preventing him from going beyond himself. Hence the curious mixture in his personality : profound spiritual craving combined with ordinary conceit ; great generosity coupled with cold indifference to other human beings, even to his friends ; certain erotic perversions, and fervent asceticism, etc. Yet the more he was aware of his own defects, the more he reacted against them by his will to realize only what was good in him. " I love all that is good. I seek it and burn with impatience to find it ; but I hate my nasty defects and do not shake hands with them as my own characters do ; I hate those base features of mine which separate me from the good. I am struggling with them. I shall drive them out, and God will help me in this."

The ethical urge of Gogol was so strong that even while he was sublimating it through his art, he gave vent to it in a more direct form—in his correspondence. The sermonizing and didactic tone was always more or less conspicuous in Gogol's letters ; it begins with those he wrote to his mother from the college. But after his triumphs, and especially during his stay abroad, he continued to preach systematically in letters to his friends. And again, he preached to them those virtues above all which he himself needed most and wished to acquire. In other words, he often forced himself to adopt certain moral attitudes at the expense of faults he wanted to get rid of. This could not interfere with his art, because his artistic creation itself was at that time largely a process of moral catharsis. No wonder that a continuous dual struggle with himself carried him often so far as to make him appear a rhetorical *poseur*. Yet even his pose was a means, not an end in itself. As one of his friends, L. T. Arnoldi (Smirnova's half-brother) remarks : " Whoever knew Gogol personally, cannot doubt the truth of Gogol's confession that he transferred the majority of his vices and weaknesses to his heroes, ridiculed them in his own writings and thus got rid of them for ever. I decidedly believe this was so. Gogol was unusually severe towards himself ; as he was struggling all the time with his own imperfections, he often fell into the other extreme and became now and then so strange and queer that many people took this for affectation and thought he was posing."

But while persecuting his defects, Gogol fell a prey to one of them : his self-assertive conceit. Like all people who doubt their own powers and are afraid of playing an inferior part in life, the part of an Akaky or Poprischin, Gogol was inclined to become authoritative and aggressive as soon as he felt power in his hands. This power had been given to him by the success of *The Revizor* and even more by that of *The Dead Souls.* Exaggerating everything that had the slightest reference to himself, he ascribed his success not to his own power (he was still not sure enough of it), but to the will of God. Transferring thus the responsibility for his own fate to God, he was inclined to see in every success a proof that a special destiny was allotted to him from on high—a destiny which was and had to be greater than that of other human beings. At last he went so far as to interpret each event of his life as a portent of God's anxious care for his person; as a sign that he was one of the elect. Yet when a man of this stamp feels elect, he certainly considers it his duty to become worthy of it: to deserve it by godly life, by prayers, by ascetic practices, and also by preaching the true path of life to those who are still groping in the darkness.

It is here that we reach the curious line where exalted religiosity and equally exalted egotism often meet and even strengthen each other, generating a kind of spiritual monomania. And what is stranger still, one's greatest inner pride may go here hand-in-hand with one's genuine tendencies towards good. The conceited self-assertive egotist and the sincerest preacher of a new life may blend to such an extent as to become almost inseparable. In Gogol, at any rate, both of them met and remained in a kind of alliance to the end of his life.

III

Gogol's own nature was certainly a favourable ground for such a combination. But quite apart from this, there were several other factors which helped, more or less, in giving his propensities such a direction.

One of them was the tragic death of Pushkin who was shot in a duel in 1837. Gogol felt that after Pushkin's death the leadership in Russian letters and culture had passed to him. But because at bottom he was diffident, as always, of his own power, he tried to emphasize his right to this leadership with all the greater passion. He took, or forced himself to take up, the whole matter even in the sense of Pushkin's *Prophet**

* Here is Mr. Maurice Baring's prose-translation of this poem which is well worth quoting: "My spirit was weary and I was athirst, and I was astray in the dark wilderness. And the Seraph with six wings appeared to me at the crossing of the ways. And he touched my eyelids, and his fingers were as soft as sleep; and like the eyes of an eagle that is frightened, my prophetic eyes were awakened. He touched my ears and he filled them with noise and with sound: and I heard the Heavens shuddering

which goes far beyond mere literature and becomes a religious task in its highest meaning ; he wanted to set God's word at the heart of Russia. Being not quite sure of his right to do so (on account of his own " nastiness ") he endeavoured to deserve it by a severe personal life and by relentless preaching to his friends of what in his opinion God Himself wanted to make manifest through him. It was at this stage that the moralizing double in him gradually became more self-conscious than ever and began to interfere with his art, trying to impose upon it " prophetic " thoughts and aims. Another important factor was the state of Gogol's health. As he could not get rid of his continuous ailments, he adopted a philosophy of life which would make him accept them, which would make him see in them even a new kind of portent from on high.

and the flight of the angels in the height, and the moving of the beasts that are under the waters, and the noise of the growth of the branches in the valley. He bent down over me and he looked upon my lips ; and he tore out my sinful tongue, and he took away that which is idle and that which is evil with his right hand, and his right hand was dabbled with blood ; and he set there in its stead, between my perishing lips, the tongue of a wise serpent. And he clove my breast asunder with a sword, and he plucked out my trembling heart, and in my cloven breast he set a burning coal of fire. Like a corpse in the desert I lay, and the voice of God called and said unto me : ' Prophet, arise and take heed and hear ; be filled with My Will and go forth over the sea and over the land and set light with My Word to the hearts of the people."

In the autumn of 1840, for instance, while staying in Vienna he had a very severe breakdown. The exact nature of his disease is not known, but to all appearance it must have been a combined ailment of the nerves and stomach, aggravated by his innate hypochondria. "To this was added a morbid melancholy for which there is no description," he says in a letter. "I was in such a state that I simply did not know where to go and what to do. I could not remain quiet even for two minutes, no matter whether I was in bed, sitting, or walking. . . . Oh, it was terrible. . . . With every day I was getting worse and worse. At last the doctor himself could not give me any hope of improvement. I understood my position, quickly gathered my energy and scribbled down as well as I could my tiny testament. But to die among Germans seemed too terrible. So I ordered a carriage and went to Italy."

Gogol may have exaggerated the whole matter, but he interpreted it again in such a way as to find in it a new proof of God's special interest in his destiny. For the graver his disease the greater must have been the miracle of his recovery—due, of course, to the direct interference of God Himself, Who wanted to preserve him for his prophetic task and mission. The same happened, but to an even greater extent, after his illness in 1845.

There were several external factors also which at that time must have partly influenced the "mystical" trend in Gogol. While in Rome he used to be a frequent guest of the Russian princess, Zinaida Volkonsky, who had become an ardent Roman Catholic.* There he met (in 1838) several Polish messianists who were fond of mixing pseudo-mystical fantasies with political utopias and aspirations. He read Mickiewicz and Krasinski, and for a while seemed rather favourably disposed towards Roman Catholicism. It was in Rome that he witnessed also the death of his young consumptive friend, Joseph Vielgorsky, perhaps the only man towards whom he ever felt unreserved friendship and also a kind of motherly tenderness, as his fragmentary lyrical jottings, *The Nights in the Villa* (1839), show. Add to this his acquaintance with the religious painter Ivanov, whose views on art were analogous to those expressed in the second version of Gogol's *Portrait*; the arrival in Rome of Zhukovsky, whose meek character had always been inclined towards the sentimental religiosity of a *schöne Seele*; and his increased friendship with Mme. Rosset-Smirnova, who suffered in her advancing years from fits of old-maidish pietism. We must mention also his closer relations

* In those days there were many other converts to Roman Catholicism among the Russian aristocrats—Prince Gagarin, Prince Meschersky, etc.

with the Moscow Slavophiles (after 1841) and with various devout ladies belonging to higher circles, ladies who were always anxious to listen to Gogol the "teacher", although socially they often considered him infinitely below themselves. Besides, occasionally one could find among them even genuine Christian souls—the old Countess Nadine Sheremetyev, for instance. Then the general homage to his genius, especially when he returned to Russia with his *Dead Souls*, must have raised even more Gogol's opinion of his own significance. Panayev (the joint Editor of the *Sovremennik*) who saw Gogol at a dinner-party during his provisional stay in Moscow, says: "He could not fail to see the worship and adoration paid to him, and he accepted all this as something due, endeavouring to conceal his satisfaction under external indifference. In his behaviour there was something strained, artificial, something that impressed painfully all those who looked upon him not as a genius but simply as a human being." The Moscow Slavophiles, in particular, began to flatter Gogol the writer to such an extent that he almost unwillingly became their *enfant gâté*, and partly even the exponent of their ideas.

In short, it was for many reasons—inner and external —that Gogol no longer contented himself with the part of a writer pure and simple, but showed a stronger and stronger wish to be a spiritual leader voicing the word and the will of God. No one who reads Gogol's letters of those years can help wondering at the rapid growth of spiritual monomania, so curiously permeated with his genuine moral aspirations. To Pogodin, for example, he wrote from Rome : "I am homeless, I am beaten and lulled by the waves, and I can lean only upon the anchor of that pride which higher powers have instilled into me. . . . You must cherish me not because of myself—no, in this vessel [*i.e.*, in Gogol] is enclosed a treasure." During the same period he wrote to another friend of his : " But listen, *now* you *must* listen to my word, because *twice* powerful is my word over you, and woe to any one who does not listen to my word . . . O, believe in my words ! Henceforth my word contains a power from on high. . . ." Once he forgot himself to such an extent as to utter this phrase : " No friend of mine can die because he will live eternally with me."

The best, although somewhat harsh, commentary on Gogol's ways at that time is perhaps the letter which Sergius Aksakov sent to him on December 9th, 1846. The letter runs as follows : " For a long time I felt dissatisfied with the trend of your religious outlook. Not that I, being a bad Christian, should have understood it badly and in consequence have feared it ; but because your Christian humility struck me as spiritual pride on your part. Many passages in your letters troubled me ; but they were expressed with such poetic brilliance, with such sincerity of feeling that I dared not obey my inner voice which condemned them, nor yet believe it ; so I endeavoured to interpret my unpleasant impressions in a manner favourable to you. I used even to be carried away and blinded by you, and I remember that once I wrote you an enthusiastic letter, genuinely grieving that I as a Christian was so immeasurably far from what I might be. Meanwhile your new outlook has developed and grown. My apprehensions were renewed with greater force : your every letter confirmed them. Instead of former friendly, warm-hearted outpourings there began to appear in them the sermonizings of a preacher, sermonizings which were mysterious, sometimes prophesying, always cold, and worst of all—full of conceit in the ragged garb of humility. I could prove these words of mine by many extracts from your letters, but I consider this would be superfluous and too painful a labour for me. Next, you sent us, together with a most puzzling letter, the soul-redeeming life of Thomas à Kempis and also detailed prescriptions as to how, when and to what extent we ought to use it ; at the same time you promised they would produce a radical change in our spiritual life. . . . My apprehension turned to downright fear, and I wrote you a rather frank and cutting letter. At that time a terrible misfortune was beginning to assail me : I was losing irretrievably the sight of one eye and had begun to feel that the other eye, too, was weakening. I was overcome with despair. I poured out my grief into your soul and received in answer a few dry and cold lines which, far from consoling and comforting the heart of an afflicted friend, only pained it.* Then you yourself were ill for a long time,** and soon after your slow recovery my agonizing sufferings began and they still continue. There were only few things in which my soul was deeply interested ; but you were always among the first. Your physical health is evidently better, and your activities have started afresh ; but what activities they are ! Each of your deeds has been a blow to me, and each one stronger than the last."

Here follow many of his frank and friendly accusations, of which I will quote only this one : " My friend, where is that Christian humility which bids us do good so that the left hand should not know what the right hand is doing ?

* Gogol consoled Aksakov with a promise of the " spiritual ' sight instead of the physical one.

** This refers to Gogol's severe illness in 1845

You are now forming, openly, and so that the whole of Russia shall hear, a Beneficent Society of your own : you are nominating its members and giving them instructions with regard to activities, which are incapable of execution and in the highest degree incompatible with anything. How could you imagine that persons whom you are appointing, especially the women, could be so indiscriminate, so immodest, as to agree to accept publicly the roles of benefactresses which you have conferred upon them ?* . . . Where is your former clear and sane notion of publicity, of ostentation in matters of beneficence ? . . . You have forgotten all about human modesty."

IV

It was during those years that the conflict between Gogol the artist and Gogol the moralist reached its climax, a conflict which has many external points of resemblance with the inner drama of Tolstoy. Full of " constructive " moral intentions, Gogol began to disapprove of the negative characters he had created in his previous

* Gogol wrote for a new edition (1846) of *The Revizor* a rather solemn preface announcing that all the money raised by it he would give to the poor, and that a special committee of aristocratic ladies, whose names were mentioned, was going to collect the money, etc.

books. He almost became haunted by them, as if they were the emanations of the Evil Spirit. Like his involuntary portrait-painter of the Devil, Gogol, too, was now tortured by the idea that his own repellent figures had perhaps been a reflection of the Evil One, and consequently a sin which must be expiated by a virtuous life, as well as by some positive and really *moral* characters that he ought to create in his new works. He intended to give us such characters in the second, and particularly in the third, part of *The Dead Souls*, in which he wanted to show a regenerated Chichikov, and even a regenerated Plyushkin.

However, it is here that we approach one of the causes of Gogol's own tragedy. We know that owing to his very constitution, his artistic vision could travel only in a romantic, or else in a ridiculing direction ; for thus he fought reality, and his own defects. No sooner had he lost this inner *raison d'être* of his art than his vision began to falter, and instead of artistic symbols he was able to give only reasoned-out moral puppets. This is what actually happened in the preserved chapters of the second part of *The Dead Souls*, which he took eleven years to write and burned twice (in 1845 and 1852). Remembering the way he had created his negative types, he felt sure that his virtuous and godly characters would not be embodied by him unless he first lived them—not in imagination only but in reality. And he began to *force* himself to live them.

This was another reason for those ascetic moods and practices to which he fell a prey during his Roman period. A reflection of his own endeavours to become worthy of his "constructive" task may be found in this passage, taken from the second version of *The Portrait* and referring to the old artist who wanted to expiate his picture of Antichrist by retiring to a cloister and taking the vows : " There he amazed everyone by the strictness of his life, and his untiring observance of all the monastic rules. The prior of the monastery, hearing of his skill in painting, ordered him to paint the principal picture in the church. But the humble brother said plainly that he was unworthy to touch a brush, that his was contaminated, that with toil and great sacrifice he must first purify his spirit in order to render himself fit to undertake such a task. He increased the rigours of monastic life for himself as much as possible. At last, even they became insufficient and he retired into the desert, in order to be quite alone. There he constructed for himself a cell from branches of trees, ate only uncooked roots, dragged about a stone from place to place, stood in one spot with his hands lifted to heaven, from the rising until the going down of the sun, reciting prayers without cessation. In this manner did he for several years exhaust his body, invigorating it at the same time with the strength of fervent prayer. At length, one day he returned to the cloister and said firmly to the prior, 'Now I am ready. If God wills, I will finish my task'."

Gogol had periods when he prepared himself in a similar way for his new work. Yet the more he forced himself, the less did he feel real and spontaneous inspiration. He could still create, in rare fits only. The unfortunate point, however, was that his lack of inspiration in a "positive" direction he now interpreted as a withdrawal of God's Grace on account of his own sinfulness. The fear of being unworthy of his great mission made him even more anxious to flagellate himself, to deserve it by prayers and fasting. "God, Who knows better than I what time is convenient for our work, has withdrawn from me, for a long period, the capacity for literary creation," he wrote to Smirnova. "I tormented myself, I compelled myself to write, I suffered heavily when I saw this helplessness of mine, and several times I made myself sick through such compulsions ; yet I was not able to do anything, and all that came out of them was artificial and bad. And often, often I was overwhelmed by ennui, and even by despair, because of this. . . ."

But as he could not esthetically visualize his own moral aspirations and ideals, he now tried to cope with them at least as a "teacher". And so, while he was writing, slowly and at intervals, the second part of his great epic, his reasoning and didactic doubles made a separate attempt to work entirely on their own. The result was a fairly voluminous book with the long title, *Selected Passages from the Correspondence with my Friends.*

This book, which appeared in 1847, consists chiefly of moral commonplaces. It is pretentious, solemn, full of the will to religion and at the same time devoid of all religious fire. Certain pages are simply tedious, for the more Gogol the moralist wishes to impose his own truths upon himself and upon others, the more rhetorical he becomes. He indulges in spiritual conceit, often talks in the tone of a law-giver ; yet with all this, many passages show that his inner quest was, nevertheless, genuine and tragic. With all its incongruities, the book is very typical of Gogol. It gives us the key to a better understanding of his self-divided nature, of his incredible inward loneliness, and of his futile attempts to get into contact with real life. His romantic temperament finds in it a new though distorted outlet, once more showing his complete inadaptability to actual existence.

Gogol himself was sure that his new book would

be a kind of revelation to his own countrymen, and perhaps also to mankind at large. Shortly before its publication, he wrote to Pletnyov (August 1846) from Schwalbach: "Here at last is my request! As a faithful friend you must fulfil this friendly request of mine. Give up all your work and get busy with the printing of this book, which has the title, *Selected Passages from the Correspondence with my Friends*. This book is needed, too much needed by all; I can say no more for the present. The rest will be explained to you by the book itself. Even before you finish printing it, everything will become clear to you, and all the doubts from which you are suffering will disappear of themselves."

No exaggeration of his own merits had ever proved so fatal to Gogol as this one. To begin with, he had no proper understanding of the social and political life of Europe or Russia; and yet he tried to solve various burning questions at one single stroke, and with that air of unperturbed competence which is so typical of ambitious dilettantes. With what self-assurance he develops there his naïve opinions about the State, the family, the Church, the Theatre, Education, about priests, landowners and officials, and even officials' wives! In a way he came—more or less independently—to certain aspects of the Slavophile doctrines, which he made as flat as possible. That is to say, Gogol stands for political quietism, for the Russian autocracy as an almost divine form of government, for serfdom, for the rigid patriarchal institutions—in a word, the whole book is a hasty jumble of social sentimentalism, combined with "pious" moods and with a distorted romantic temper which crops up in various forms of moral monomania simply because here it finds its line of least resistance. As a panacea for all evils, he preaches personal influence and persuasion through logic, and in this too he resembles the "converted" Tolstoy, although the inner motives of Tolstoy's moralism were different from those of Gogol.* Some of his thoughts (those on the Theatre, for example) may be sound, but the final impression one obtains from the book as a whole is that Gogol was not a thinker and did not comprehend the spirit of the age which he wished to reform. Even that Russia in which he once lived seemed to have entirely escaped from him. And what is worse, he tried to justify, as it were, that very system of Russian life which he had previously attacked in *The Revizor* and in the first part of *The Dead Souls*.

One of his Russian critics, Ivanov-Razumnik, aptly observes that Gogol, who was by his very

* The problem of Tolstoy is dealt with in my book, *Tolstoy* (Collins).

nature a great anti-philistine, finished by falling into ethical philistinism. When he was about to celebrate the victory of his self-conquest, he was already a victim, and wrote, moreover, an apotheosis of ordinary bourgeois existence, reducing life in the best case to a stale patriarchial idyll in the manner of his old-world landowners who thrived so well on the labour of their serfs. Yet, taken as a whole, the *Correspondence* is a reliable picture of Gogol's inner state at that time. His " philistinism " was the result of his own inner blind-alley. When he wanted to be a prophet he had no prophetic vision whatever. This is confirmed also by the second part of *The Dead Souls*. For the ideals of its positive characters, such as Murazov and Skudrozhoglo, do not go beyond those of the acquisitive bourgeois. True, the swindler Chichikov dreams of moral regeneration, but only of such a one which would enable him to become, in all safety, a wealthy and even respected landowner. " Chichikov could not sleep. His thoughts were wide awake. The possibility of becoming rich seemed so evident, the difficult work of managing an estate seemed to have become so easy and intelligible, and seemed so well suited to his temperament, that he began to think seriously of obtaining not an imaginary, but a real estate. He at once determined, with the money he would get by mortgaging the imaginary souls, to obtain an estate that would not be imaginary. He already saw himself managing his estate and doing everything as Skudrozhoglo had instructed him, promptly, carefully, introducing nothing new until he had thoroughly mastered everything old, looking into everything with his own eyes, getting to know all his peasantry, rejecting all superfluities, devoting himself to nothing but work, and looking after his land. . . . He had already a foretaste of the delight that he would feel when he had introduced harmonious order, when every part of the organization was moving briskly and working well together. The work would go merrily, and just as the flour is swiftly ground out of the grain in the mill, it would grind all sorts of rubbish and refuse into ready money. His marvellous host rose before his imagination every moment. He was the first man in all Russia for whom he had felt a personal respect."

This was written by Gogol in no way ironically, but in perfect seriousness, and quite in the spirit of his *Correspondence*. As the latter deals with many aspects of individual and social life, it would be interesting to quote some of his advice, such as this, for example (from the " Letter to a Landowner ") : " Your remarks concerning schools are quite right. To give a peasant a school-education in order to enable him to read empty booklets published by our European humanitarians is sheer nonsense. Besides, a peasant has no time for this. . . ." Equally biased are most of his views on politics, on religion, on the official Church. They breathe at times such a reactionary spirit that the consumptive Bielinsky could not refrain from addressing to him the most indignant and passionate letter he had ever written.

"You were only partly right in seeing in my article an angered man," he wrote to Gogol from Salzbrunn ; "this epithet is too weak and tender to express that condition into which the reading of your book had plunged me. . . . One can bear the feeling of wounded pride, but it is impossible to bear the feeling of outraged truth, of outraged humanity. It is impossible to keep silent when under the cloak of religion and under the protection of the knout, lies and immorality are being preached as truth and virtue. And you say that such a book could have been the result of a difficult inner process, of high spiritual illumination ! Either you are ill—and you must quickly undergo a cure, or . . . I dare not pronounce my thought ! . . . . You preacher of the knout, apostle of ignorance, defender of obscurantism and darkest oppression, you eulogist of Tartar manners—what are you doing ! Look beneath your feet—you are standing over an abyss. . . . I can well understand why you base your doctrine on the Orthodox Church: she was always a supporter of the knout and a flatterer of despotism; but for what reason do you mix up Christ with all this? What have you found in common between Him and any Church, especially the Orthodox one? He was the first to announce to men the doctrine of freedom, of equality and brotherhood, and He sealed the sincerity of His teaching with His own martyrdom. His teaching had remained salvation of men only until it became organized into a Church and based on dogmas. And the Church itself became hierarchic, that is to say, a defender of inequality, a flatterer of power, an enemy and pursuer of brotherhood among men—which she continues to be also in our days. . . . As to the humility which you are preaching, in the first place, it is not new; and secondly, it savours of a fearful conceit on the one side, and of a shameful abasement of your human dignity on the other. The idea of becoming some kind of abstract perfection, of rising above all others through one's humility can be the fruit either of conceit or of idiocy, and in both cases it invariably leads to hypocrisy, cant and stagnation. Apart from this, you took the liberty of cynically slandering, in your book, not only others (which in itself would be only uncivil), but also your own person, which is disgusting ; for if a man who strikes his own fellow-being in the face arouses indignation, a man striking his own face arouses contempt. No, you are only bemused and not enlightened ; you have understood neither the form nor the spirit of contemporary Christianity. It is not the truth of Christian teaching that your book breathes but the fear of death, of the devil and of hell."

V

It was not only Bielinsky who attacked Gogol. Once again, all turned against him. The religious Slavophiles accused him of spiritual pride, the Westerners of reactionary views. The book made a tremendous stir chiefly because the whole of the Russian intelligentsia, including Gogol's personal friends, were against it.

Gogol had, of course, hoped the influence of his *Correspondence* would surpass everything that had been written before in Russia. He thought it would be accepted by all and sundry as a second Bible. Instead of this he suddenly met with attacks, with derision, and with absolute misunderstanding even of the good points of the book which had been either overlooked or misinterpreted. The only benevolent attitude was that of the Russian government, and this alone was enough to ruin the reputation of any writer.

In the same way as he always used to exaggerate his success, Gogol now magnified his failure. He suddenly lost his " prophetic " zest, his self-assurance, and tried to beat a retreat in every possible direction. And so his excuses became rather contradictory. In a private letter from Naples (May 1847) he defends himself with these lines : " In spite of all the great defects of my book, there is in it nevertheless one truth which so far has been noticed only by few people. It represents the drama of a soul—the confession of a man who has begun to feel that our education starts only at that point where you would think it has already finished. . . . If anyone begins even only to think of becoming better, he will throw my book away and take the Gospel. . . . I repeat, the intention of my book was a good one. But you see now how much I still need to be prayed for, more than any other man. If God does not enlighten me with His own understanding, what will become of me ? My fate will be more terrible than that of other beings. For the sake of Christ, do pray for me."

He was quite sincere in this letter. Yet he was equally sincere when writing to Zhukovsky : " I displayed in my book so much of my own Khlestakov-nature that I do not dare even to glance at it. . . . How ashamed I am of myself, how ashamed I feel before you, good soul! I feel ashamed of having imagined that my school-education was already finished and that I could be equal to you. Truly, there is something of Khlestakov in me. . . ." In his defence he soon began to use almost every argument he could get hold of. He even stated that he had published that unfortunate work not in order to teach, but in order to be taught by other people's opinions about it. . . . His *Author's Confession* was a kind of self-justification in this sense. At the same time he wrote to S. Aksakov (July, 1847) these valuable words: "Impatience made me publish my book. Seeing that I would not be able to master my *Dead Souls* and genuinely grieving over the colourlessness of modern literature, which indulges in empty discussions, I hastened to say a word on the problems I was interested in and which I had wanted to develop, or create in living images and characters."

But all things considered, the gap between Gogol's expectations and the actual result of the book was more than he could bear. The blow made him fall from extreme pride to extreme despondence. Weary, full of renewed doubts, disappointed and wavering, he began a revision of his inner life, trying to look at himself more objectively than before. This letter to Aksakov written from Frankfort (June 10th, 1847), says more than any analysis could ever say : " For the sake of Christ Himself, put yourself in my place in order to get an idea of how difficult it is, and tell me : what am I to do ? How and what am I now to write ? If I had the power of saying a sincere word, my very tongue would remain tied. In sincere language one can speak only to those who have at least some faith in our sincerity ; but if you are dealing with a man who has already formed his own opinion of you and persists in it, then even the sincerest person will remain dumb, and not only I who am reserved (as you know) and whose very reserve arises from my inability to explain myself. For the sake of Christ Himself I beg you now, not in the name of friendship, but in the name of that charity which is to be found in every good and compassionate soul—in the name of charity, I beg you to put yourself in my place, because my heart is torn with grief, however much I try to be brave and calm. My relations with all those friends of mine who hastened to make friends with me before they got to know me have become too painful. I myself am at a loss to understand how it is that I have not yet gone mad from all this humbug. All I know is that my heart is broken and my will to action paralyzed. It is still possible to struggle with infuriated foes, but God preserve us from the terrible battle with our friends. Everything that is in man gets broken by it. My friend, I am broken—this is all I can say for the present. But in so far as the constancy of my affections is concerned, this much I will say, that my soul is more open to love than ever before. If I love and wish to love even those who do not love me, how should I then not love those who do love me? But it is not love that I beg of you now. Give me not your love, but give me at least a drop of your pity, because I repeat, my position is difficult. If you really put yourself in my place you would see that I suffer more than all those whom I have offended. My friend, all I tell you is true."

This letter is perhaps the best introduction to the last phase of Gogol's life, which is even more curious and more tragic than its previous phases.

Chapter Eight

GOGOL'S LAST YEARS

I

THE last few years of Gogol's life could best be defined as a ceaseless inner crisis, the result of which was almost a complete arrest of his literary creation. His Italian sojourn had at first a good effect on him, but as his inner fight went on, he was driven to continuous preoccupation with himself, with his own spiritual dangers, temptations and problems. This led him to an even greater estrangement from life, from people, from art itself. He ceased to enjoy even Italy. His "lovely, far-away paradise" lost its former magic for him. He felt lonely in this world, lonely when alone, and even lonelier when among people. His occasional outbursts of imaginary enthusiasm and gaiety usually ended in grey apathy, which was now invading Gogol's soul like a creeping paralysis.

Sollogub gives this account of Gogol's later

years abroad : " He stood aloof and avoided society ; it seems that only once in his life he had put on a black dress-coat, and even then not his own—this happened when he received an invitation from the Grand Duchess Maria Nikolayevna to visit her in Rome. Gogol's reserve amounted almost to eccentricity. He was not afraid of people but he found them a nuisance. No sooner had a visitor arrived than he used to disappear from his room. But now and then he could still be gay ; he would read in the evenings his works, always the printed ones only, or impersonate, amongst others, his former Nyezhin teachers so comically that the onlookers would burst with laughter. Yet his life was severe and sad. In the morning he read John Chrysostom, he wrote, and then tore up all he had written ; he walked a great deal and was now sublimely simple, now incredibly queer."

Feeling more and more tormented, disgusted and utterly uprooted, he hardly knew how to defend himself against that inner torpor which lames even the richest souls—leaving in them only frost and tedium. Already in his *Correspondence* he gave us a glimpse into this mood when—amongst all his sermonizing rhetoric—he suddenly exclaimed, as if from the depths : " And our earth has become aflame with incomprehensible ennui ; harder and harder is life ; steadily it becomes more and more petty ; and before the eyes of all there grows only the gigantic figure of boredom ; it grows and assumes infinite dimensions every day. O Lord ! Empty and terrible becomes Thy world ! " Amongst many other reasons, it was the fear of this emptiness that drove Gogol to his teaching and preaching. Parallel with the wish to gratify his moral egotism, he must have cherished some hope that his growing tedium could be overcome only by a great mission. This hope was, however, entirely shattered by the failure of his *Correspondence*. And what is worse, that very public among which he wished to play the part of a prophet turned against him with an almost perverted cruelty, thus undermining Gogol's faith in himself at the very moment when his creative capacities, too, were slowly deserting him. And so all his doubts, his vacillation and weakness assailed him more than ever, while his loneliness began to pass into that icy indifference which is worse than death.

Nothing but profound religious fire could perhaps still save Gogol from himself. Unfortunately, when he most needed such fire, he noticed with horror that he had none : true religion was lacking in Gogol as much as it was lacking—forty years later—in the converted Tolstoy. Instead of spontaneous religiosity we see in him only " religious " intellect (which led him to moralizing), or "religious" imagination, which led him to superstitious fears and perhaps even to actual visions of the devil. However, like Tolstoy, Gogol too had a desperate will to religion ; and this will was all the more sincere the more he suspected his own lack of religion. His exaggerated piety and asceticism were often due to his desperate though futile desire to become truly and genuinely religious. He lacerated himself inwardly, prayed, fasted ; he even thought of becoming a monk ; he composed a quasi-mystical *Meditation on the Divine Liturgy*,* but all was in vain. And from the people, from his own countrymen and friends, he saw now nothing but misunderstandings. For even a man like Bielinsky was right, and was not right, when passing his severe sentence on him and his *Correspondence*. What else could he do but exclaim in his tragic isolation : "If I could find one soul only ! If only one soul would wish to speak to me ! Everything seems to have died out. I think only dead souls still exist in Russia. It is dreadful."

In such a frame of mind he tried his last medium against the slow death of his own soul : he went to Palestine in the hope of rousing himself in the most sacred places of the earth.

* Begun in 1845, left incomplete and published only five years after his death.

LAST YEARS

II

Gogol had been contemplating this journey for quite a long time and from various contradictory inner motives. He started it early in 1848, *i.e.*, after all the troubles and disappointments connected with his *Correspondence*. He started it as an invalid who goes to a shrine in search of a miraculous cure. Only a few weeks before his departure, Gogol wrote from Naples to one of his new acquaintances, Father Matthew (24 Dec., 1847) : " I am not sure whether I shall give up literature, because I don't know whether such be the will of God ; in any case, my reason tells me not to publish anything for a long time until I get more mature—inwardly and spiritually. But meanwhile I am going to Jerusalem to pray at our Saviour's Tomb, to pray as much as I can. Do pray for me, good soul, so that I myself shall be able to pray fervently and deeply. Do pray to God that in the very place where His divine Son had been treading, my heart should reveal to me all I need to do. I wish that from the very day of that worship of mine I should carry the image of Christ in my heart wherever I go, and that I should have Him all the time before my soul's eyes."

However full of hope this letter may be, it

shows that it was not real spontaneous piety, but despair at the coldness of his own heart that drove Gogol to Jerusalem. Besides, he himself confessed this in another letter to the same person (12, II, 1848): "Alas, it is not easy to pray. How can one pray if God does not want you to? I see so much that is bad in me, such an abyss of self-love and incapacity to sacrifice earthly things for the sake of the heavenly principle. . . . Only now I am surprised at my own conceit, wondering how it is that God has not struck me and wiped me off the face of the earth. O my friend, my confessor, whom God Himself has sent to me! I am burning with shame and don't know where to hide my face—so much am I now overwhelmed by the incredible quantity of my weaknesses and vices which I did not even suspect before. And here is my confession—no longer with regard to my authorship! I could write entire pages about my pusillanimity, superstition, fear. It even seems to me that I have no religion. I confess Christ only because my reason and not my religion commands me to do so. . . . *I only wish to believe*, and in spite of this I now dare to go on a pilgrimage to our Saviour's Tomb. Oh, do pray for me. . . ."

Having once reached Jerusalem, Gogol summoned all that was best in him. He tried to abandon himself to fervent prayers, to stir up all his dormant feelings, all his will to religion—but the result was just the reverse from what he had expected. The miracle of inner transformation did not take place. In the depth of his soul he still remained unmoved and frozen, as it were. He remained entirely cold even at our Saviour's Tomb. And when stopping for a couple of rainy days in Nazareth, his mood was that of a man waiting at a dreary postal station in the Russian provinces. Dissatisfied with himself, he travelled a little in Syria, where he was joined by his former school comrade, Basili. As Basili had an influential diplomatic post in those parts, he did his best to help the great writer. The nervous Gogol proved, however, a bad companion. In spite of all his assumed humility, he treated his kind friend as if the latter were his servant ; he shouted at him and gesticulated hysterically at the smallest displeasure. Seeing that Gogol might compromise his prestige among the natives, Basili considered it necessary to react in the proper way, that is, as a master. The result was that Gogol at once became meek and silent. Otherwise nothing important happened during his stay in Palestine. Yet the things that were going on within his own soul must have been terrible.

It was Bielinsky who said in his famous one-sided letter to Gogol : " One can pray anywhere, and only those people go to search after Christ in

Jerusalem who either have never had Him in their hearts or who have lost Him. Those who can suffer at the sight of other people's suffering ; those who feel personally oppressed when others are being oppressed, carry Christ in their hearts, and consequently there is no reason why they should go to Jerusalem." In these lines Bielinsky put his finger on the sore spot of Gogol's religious quest. He guessed his secret ; but he hardly realized how complex and how painful this secret must have been to Gogol himself, particularly to that Gogol who wished to find in religion a haven from his inner chaos and could not reach it. Knowing that the Kingdom of God cannot be conquered by force, since it is given only as a gift, he had done everything a man can do to obtain it by the Grace of God : he had repented, he had prayed, he had fasted, he had gone to Jerusalem. Yet as the gift from on high was not forthcoming and his soul did not melt, he was bound (with his turn of mind) to consider his failure a sign that God did not want him, and that he was rejected, doomed. Christ Himself was silent when Gogol knelt all night praying at His Tomb, praying for inner regeneration, as well as for a living tie between himself and the world in which he had to live.

It was his Palestine journey that increased his fears of being condemned and of falling into the power of the devil—of the *real* devil, in whom Gogol believed with the atavistic belief of a peasant. Some of the letters he wrote on his return from Jerusalem are heart-rending. To Father Matthew, for example, he acknowledged quite frankly in his message from Odessa (April, 1848) : " I must tell you that never before had I been so little pleased with the state of my own soul as in Jerusalem and after Jerusalem. I only had the opportunity of seeing more clearly than ever my hardness, my self-love—that's the whole result." And to Zhukovsky (Feb., 1850) : " I was fortunate enough to spend a whole night at our Saviour's Tomb, to communicate there, and yet I did not become better than I was." To that truly Christian friend of his, the Countess Nadine Sheremetyev, he wrote again (May, 1848) from his village Vassilyevka, where he stopped for a time after his pilgrimage : " God be thanked, I have reached my earthly home without any mishap ; but shall I reach in the same way my heavenly home ? This is the question which ought to occupy me at present entirely. To my own shame I must confess that my soul is far from this question. My head thinks of it, but my soul does not melt nor does it become aflame with the yearning for *that*. It looks as if I had been at the Tomb of our Saviour only in order to feel *there*, on that very spot, how terribly cold my soul is, and how egotistic and self-loving. And so that which I thought was *near* is *far away* now. . . . With cold lips, and with a hard soul, I continue to lisp the same prayer and in the same way as before. . . . My friend, do pray for me."

III

After his journey to the Holy Land he stayed a few weeks in the Ukraine, but in the autumn of the same year he went to Moscow. One of those who saw him in Moscow at the end of 1848, N. V. Berg, describes him as " a little man, with a small moustache, with quick and penetrating dark eyes and somewhat pale. With his hands in his pockets, he walked to and fro, and spoke. His gait was original, mincing, and not quite sure —as if one leg continually wanted to jump forward, in consequence of which one step always came out longer than the other. In his entire figure there was something fettered, tied and utterly suppressed. He showed no ease, no frankness, either in his looks or gestures. On the contrary, the looks he cast about at random were not direct and straightforward, but sidelong, occasional, and evasive as it were." Melchior de Vogüé depicts him (in his *Roman Russe*), on the testimony of an eye-witness, in these terms :

" He was small in stature ; his legs too short in proportion to his body, with a crooked walk ; shy and badly set. A mass of hair like a horse's mane well down over his forehead, and his long, prominent nose made him look rather ridiculous. He spoke very little and with difficulty. Now and then he recovered some of his former brightness, especially when with children, who were always dear to him : but he soon relapsed into his habitual gloom." And Sollogub gives us this account of his last meeting with Gogol : " I saw Gogol for the last time in 1850, in Moscow. He came to say good-bye to me and began to talk so disconnectedly, in such a vague and obscure manner, that I became alarmed and confused. When I said something about the originality of Moscow, Gogol's face became brighter, a spark of his former gaiety flashed into his eyes, and he told me in his own Gogolian fashion an extremely interesting and typical anecdote. But immediately after the anecdote he became sad again and entangled himself in such confused speech that I realized he was past recovery."

It must have been in a similar state that Gogol, the incurable egotist, tried to get away from his ego by submitting definitely to a man whose influence was fatal to him. This man was Father Matthew Konstantinovsky—a rough and fanatical priest from Rzhev, who had previously "distinguished" himself by his merciless persecution of Russian dissenters. Gogol was recommended to him in 1847 (while still abroad) by a former procurator of the Holy Synod—Count A. P. Tolstoy—and sent him a copy of his *Correspondence*. Father Matthew answered, however, with an indignant letter in which he raged, above all, against Gogol's favourable attitude towards the Theatre. Soon after his return from Palestine, Gogol met Father Matthew personally. Ivan Scheglov, who has dedicated several interesting pages to the study of this figure, gives us an almost incredible account of the first meeting between Gogol and the reverend Father.

"What is your religion?" was the priest's stern question when Gogol was introduced to him.

"Orthodox."

"You are not a Protestant?"

"No, I am not a Protestant. Certainly not. I am Orthodox. . . . I am Gogol. . . ."

"In my eyes you are simply a swine," retorted the pious Father Matthew. "What kind of an Orthodox Christian are you if you do not beg of me God's Grace and my pastoral blessing! . . ."

Such records must not be accepted without reserve. Yet with all due caution we can say that the quoted scene is quite likely to have taken place. Although the reports about Father

Matthew vary, we can sum up his general characteristics by saying that he was one of those primitive natures who are made of one piece, and who go in one direction simply because their inner life is not differentiated at all. It is their narrowness which makes them strong in their will and in their morals. Both his will and his morals were, in fact, ruthless. He was dogmatically sure of himself, unflinching in his severe way of life ; but his very asceticism might have been a disguise for his spiritual lust for power. Gogol himself wanted to teach and tyrannize over others because he was never quite sure of his own strength and value : he was fond of worshippers and adoration because he needed continuous external proofs of his own significance in order to believe in it. With Father Matthew, however, things were different. Being an obstinate and extremely self-willed masculine nature, he never doubted his own power, and he probably exercised it over others with the perverted enjoyment of an Inquisitor.

No wonder that Gogol, the wavering and will-less Gogol, with his complex inner life, was fascinated by this " holy " priest, who seemed so sure of himself and of his own truth. In the end he entirely surrendered his will to him—to the extent of becoming his obedient tool. Father Matthew was the anchor to which he continued to clutch as if afraid of going to the bottom after all his shattered hopes and illusions. The pious man's domineering instinct could now rejoice : a recognized genius, a celebrated author known all over Russia, was in his spiritual grip. And why should he not get hold of him as completely as possible ? In fact, he soon discovered Gogol's weak points and acted accordingly. Seeing the intensity of Gogol's fear of the Beyond, he endeavoured to " save " him by influencing his imagination, that is, by talking of hell and hell-fire. His descriptions of the tortures inflicted upon the condemned souls were so glowing and vivid that on one occasion Gogol shivered like a child and shouted at the holy man, " Enough ! Enough ! "

The strangest thing about it, however, is that consciously Father Matthew was quite sincere and serious about Gogol's salvation. Moreover, he might have grieved about Gogol's " sins " as bitterly as Gogol himself. Severe in his exhortations, he was perhaps all the more affectionate in his ordinary intercourse with him, the more he wanted to subdue him spiritually. And he subdued him in every respect. He had such power over him that he dared to interfere even with his artistic creation, proclaiming it as godless and pernicious. The pious fanatic had not read any of his works except the *Selected Passages from the*

Correspondence (of which he disapproved), yet he wanted to be the only competent judge of Gogol the artist. And since the unfortunate author submitted in all things, why should he waver in this respect ?

IV

It is, of course, difficult to say in how far this man was responsible for Gogol's final catastrophe, but he certainly did aggravate his state of mind. Since all other means of salvation had defied Gogol, art might again perhaps have provided a haven for him, a haven in which he could forget himself and the world ; but this outlet, too, was now barred by his spiritual guide—for moral reasons. Yet, in spite of Father Matthew's exhortations, Gogol was not able to give up entirely either writing or his interest in art. Soon after his return to Moscow (in 1848) he revived his former study of folk-songs, whose fascination he could never resist. He immersed himself in various *byliny* and *dumy*. He even learned Serbian in order to read the Jugoslav folk-ballads, the beauty of which had found ardent admirers in such men as Goethe and Grimm. He continued, moreover, to work at the second part of *The Dead Souls*, all the time trying to blend his artistic vision with his moralizing purpose. But, like Tolstoy, he too was able to mix them only, without blending them at all, as we can see in the preserved five chapters of the second part. Many pages of these chapters are magnificent, although they probably do not represent the final version of the work. But from reliable witnesses we know that such a version did exist. While in Kaluga, Gogol read a few of its chapters to Mme. Rosset-Smirnova and to her half-brother Arnoldi.* On August 29th, 1849, he read its first chapter to Aksakov. According to Pletnyov, in the summer of 1851 seven chapters were read by Gogol to a gathering of several people. N. V. Berg again mentions eleven chapters which were ready, in that year, for publication. Moreover, all those who had heard various portions of this work assert with unfeigned enthusiasm that they were excellent.

In several passages of the preserved fragments we can feel the powerful pen of the former Gogol. Yet in it we would seek in vain for new spiritual horizons. Incapable of any visions which would provide an outlet, the tired Gogol seems to be looking backwards : like his Hans Küchelgarten, Gogol returns—in his yearnings, at any rate—to the snug patriarchal idyll of his youth. More tired than Hans, disappointed and beaten by life,

* Arnoldi relates (in the *Russky Viestnik*, I, 1862) the lost contents of these chapters.

he longs only for a refuge where he would be left in peace by all. He cannot help sympathizing even with Chichikov when he makes him dream of a similar refuge—in the shape of an idyllic country estate. Take this description of Chichikov's moods after the row, arranged by his host, Pyetuh, on the river :

" Meanwhile the sun had set, the sky remained clear and transparent. There was the sound of shouting. In place of the fishermen there were groups of boys bathing on the banks ; splashing and laughter echoed in the distance. The oarsmen, after plying their twenty-four oars in unison, suddenly raised them all at once into the air, and the long boat, light as a bird, darted of itself over the motionless, mirror-like surface. A fresh-looking, sturdy lad, the third from the stern, began singing in a clear voice ; five others caught it up and the other six joined in and the song followed on, endless as Russia ; and putting their hands to their oars, the singers themselves seemed lost in endlessness. Listening to it one felt free and at ease, and Chichikov thought : 'Ah, I really shall have a country place of my own one day.'

" It was dusk as they returned. In the dark the oars struck the water which no longer reflected the sky. Lights were visible on both sides of the river. The moon rose just as they were touching the bank. On all sides fishermen were boiling soup of perch and still quivering fish on tripods. Everything was at home. The geese, the cows and the goats had been driven home long before, and the very dust raised by them was laid again by now, and the herdsmen who had driven them were standing by the gates waiting for a jug of milk and an invitation to partake of fish soup. Here and there came the sound of talk and the hum of voices, the loud barking of the dogs of their village, and of other villages far away. The moon had risen and had begun to light up the darkness ; and at last everything was bathed in light—the lake and the huts ; the light of the fires was paler ; the smoke from the chimneys could be seen silvery in the moonlight. . . . 'Oh, I really will have an estate of my own one day,' thought Chichikov. A buxom wife and little Chichikovs rose before his imagination again. Whose heart could not have been warmed by such an evening ! "

V

An idyllic existence of this kind might have been granted eventually to the " regenerated " Chichikov, but it was never granted to Gogol. Driven by his own inner chaos, he was doomed to remain a sad and homeless wanderer even during the last years of his life. For he was now deserted even by his creative power, which alone perhaps could still give him a few moments of forgetfulness and rapture. "What is this," he wrote to Zhukovsky in December, 1849, "old age or temporary paralysis of my forces? . . . My creative faculty is lazy. I am doing my best not to lose a single minute; I hardly ever leave my writing table with sheets of paper on it, but the lines I write shape themselves in a sluggish way. Or is it possible that I am really an old man at the age of forty-two?"

But he had still one remedy left—the "long, long road." He roamed for a while in Russia, unhappy, restless, and as though pursued by an invisible foe. But finding no peace, no contact with real life, he came back again to Moscow, where he was put up by Count A. Tolstoy. His host did everything to enliven Gogol's moods, but with no great success. Fits of melancholy were sometimes succeeded by fits of gaiety, which became more and more rare. Quite apart from the sinister influence of his confessor, Father Matthew, he was gradually succumbing to his own hypochondria, to his fear of death and eternal damnation. This fear overpowered him particularly in January, 1852—owing to the death of one of his friends (Mme. Homyakov). He soon showed symptoms of mental trouble.

Frightened by the sudden death of his friend, he began to prepare himself for his own death. In order to propitiate God, he started praying day and night. He exhausted his body by fasting. In his expectation of the eternal Judge he looked like a walking ghost. Truth, life, God and mankind—they all seemed far away from him, somewhere above him, and he had not the proper ladder to reach them. He also suffered from hallucinations, and their effect must have been proportionate to the intense vividness of his own imagination. "Have mercy on me, O Lord! Bind the Satan again through the power of the mysterious Cross!" These lines he jotted down only a few days before he died.

In the night of February 11th, 1852, he prayed with exceptional fervour. Then he got up, called his boy-servant and, with a candle in his hand, wandered through his rooms, crossing himself in each of them. Suddenly he took out of his portfolio a bundle of manuscripts, put most of it into the fireplace, and set it on fire with his own candle. The boy probably guessed what was the matter, and implored him in tears to spare the manuscripts. "This is not your business—you must pray," answered Gogol. He waited until all the sheets had turned into ashes, crossed himself, kissed the boy, and went to his bedroom, where he fell upon the divan and began to cry.

Among the manuscripts he had thus destroyed was the completed second part of the *Dead Souls*. However, the whole incident still remains a mystery. Did he act in a sudden fit of semi-madness, or was he entirely conscious of what he was doing ? And if Gogol did all this deliberately, what were his inner motives ? Was it the greatest triumph over his own pride, or the greatest and final pride triumphant over him ? Or did he wish to burn a few chapters only, and by mistake destroyed more than he had intended ? Or had he burned the MS., genuinely convinced that he would write the whole of it again, and better ? However this may be, he gave a mystifying, or at least evasive, explanation to his host, A. P. Tolstoy. " Fancy how powerful the Evil Spirit is ! " he said to him. " I wanted to burn some papers which were intended to be destroyed ; but instead of this I burned the chapters of my *Dead Souls*, which I wished to leave to my friends in memory of my death."

Soon after this he refused to eat altogether. On February 21st, 1852, he died from exhaustion. His last words were, " Give me the ladder, the ladder ! " And—who knows ?—in their own way they are perhaps as symbolic as the words of the dying Goethe : " More light ! More light ! "

Chapter Nine

CONCLUSION

As neither scope nor space allows me to touch upon the more detailed aspects of Gogol's work, something must be said at least about its influence and significance. This is all the more necessary because, quite apart from being one of the greatest masters of the word, Gogol is beyond any doubt a unique representative of that strange period when European romanticism was gradually passing into what is called realism. As we have seen, there is no strict dividing line between these two trends of Gogol's art : in his case, they are but two aspects of one and the same attitude towards the world and life. And so, however plausible his "realistic" methods may look on the surface, we must not forget that they are the best and most elusive mask of his essentially romantic nature.

Everything in this man is elusive, unexpected, paradoxical. There is something paradoxical even in the part he plays in the *belles lettres* of his own country ; for Gogol influenced Russian literature by what he seemed to be, rather than by what he was. Thus owing to the fact that he had been mistaken for a realist *pur sang*, especially by Bielinsky, he helped above all in promoting the realistic orientation among the writers of the subsequent period. And he did this in many directions. Some of his works, such as *The Revizor*, are largely responsible for the accusatory note ; others—*The Cloak*, for example—for the note of pity in which the leaders of the " natural school " often indulged more than necessary ; others again for that exquisite *Kleinmalerei* which is the great secret of so many Russian writers.

Yet Gogol's profound and somewhat distorted subjectivity could not pass unnoticed either. It certainly affected some of the younger authors, particularly Dostoevsky, whose first stories, *The Poor Folk* and *The Double*, are direct descendants of Gogol's *Cloak* and *A Madman's Diary*. V. Rozanov goes even so far as to lay upon Gogol the entire responsibility for the " ironical trend ", for the cult of subjectivism, and also for that spite against reality which was so strong in both the literature and the intelligentsia of his country. But whether we agree with Rozanov or not, one thing is certain : that the whole of Russian literature fluctuates between the great and simple obectivity bequeathed to it by Pushkin, and that morbid subjectivism which received its first impulse from Gogol. Tolstoy, Turgenev and Goncharov took their artistic methods from Pushkin, while the young Dostoevsky adopted not only Gogol's morbidity, but also his nervous, exuberant style, and even his hyperbolism, which he transferred from the physical to the psychological plane.

On the whole, Gogol made his influence felt more by detached single elements of his writings than by the sum of his work. "All that is really alive and vital in the currents of our literature explains him, or even is explained by him. Gogol's full and elemental artistic nature is being directed into various channels by our contemporary authors." Thus wrote the gifted critic, Apollon Grigoryev, in 1852, and he was partly right, at any rate with regard to his own generation.

Had not the talent of Sergius Aksakov ripened and given its best owing to his contact with the art of Gogol? Gogol's social satire found an eager follower in Saltykov-Schedrin. Ostrovsky again developed his dramatic gift under the influence of Gogol's plays. Even those writers who were leaning on Pushkin could not help borrowing to some extent from Gogol. Goncharov, for instance, elaborated the antithesis of Tentetnikov and Skudrozhoglo in the two main characters—Oblomov and Stolz—of his best novel. Certain features of Gogol's art can also be traced at times in Chehov, and even as far down as Andrey Biely, who is often too much under the spell of his rhythmic and ornamental style. This quality of Gogol's prose seems to affect—mainly through Biely—some of the youngest, post-revolutionary authors—whether with benefit or not, it is difficult to say.

On the other hand, the very dilemma of Gogol the writer is in many ways typical of Russian literature with its inwardly restless and *seeking* trend. Is not Tolstoy's inner drama a replica of the drama of Gogol? Dostoevsky's passionate search, too, reminds us, now and then, of Gogol's own quest. Even the pessimism of Gogol is strikingly " Russian " in so far as it is but the inversion of his unquenchable thirst after a higher form of life both individual and social.

This inner thirst is so imperious in some of the outstanding Russian authors that in their best works they are usually more concerned about great life than about great art—a tendency which makes them strive after a plane where art grows not apart from man, but together with him. The ultimate tragedy of Gogol was that he could not attain to such a plane—since Gogol the artist was so immeasurably greater than Gogol the man. And he had to pay a big price for this discrepancy:

entangled in his own inner difficulties, he was wrecked at last both as man and as artist. He was a victim of his own impossible craving—the craving to reach that point where great art and great life meet and merge into one.

CHRONOLOGICAL LIST OF GOGOL'S WORKS

1829. HANS KUCHELGARTEN.

1830. WOMAN.

ST. JOHN'S EVE. (Printed for the first time anonymously in THE ANNALS OF THE FATHERLAND.)

1831. CHAPTER FROM A HISTORICAL NOVEL.

THE SCHOOLMASTER. A SUCCESSFUL MISSION (both from the unfinished story, THE FEARFUL BOAR, printed in THE LITERARY JOURNAL).

THE EVENINGS ON A FARM NEAR DIKANKA. (*Vechera na Khutorve Bliz Dikanki.*)

First Part, including the following stories:

1. The Fair of Sorochintsy.
2. St. John's Eve.
3. The May Night.
4. The Lost Letter.

1832. THE EVENINGS ON A FARM NEAR DIKANKA.

Second Part, including the following stories:

1. Christmas Eve.
2. Cruel Vengeance.
3. Ivan Shponka and his Aunt.
4. The Bewitched Spot.

1835. ARABESQUES: A Collection of Essays, which includes the stories:

1. Nevsky Prospekt.
2. A Madman's Diary.
3. The Portrait.
4. The Prisoner.

MIRGOROD. First Part, including:

1. The Oldworld Landowners.
2. Taras Bulba.

Second Part, including:

1. Viy.
2. The Story of the Quarrel between Ivan Ivanovitch and Ivan Nikiforovitch.

1836. THE NOSE.
THE CARRIAGE.
REVIZOR.
PETERSBURG NOTES.
MOVEMENT OF OUR JOURNALISTIC LITERATURE IN 1834-1835.

1842. THE PORTRAIT, in its re-made form. (Published in *Sovremennik*).
DEAD SOULS. First Volume. (Published on May 21st, in St. Petersburg.)

In the autumn of the same year appeared the first collection of his works (in four volumes). It includes:

THE EVENINGS, MIRGOROD (with the final version of TARAS BULBA); THE PORTRAIT, THE NEVSKY PROSPECT, A MADMAN'S DIARY, ROME, THE NOSE, THE CARRIAGE, THE CLOAK, THE MARRIAGE, THE GAMBLERS, THE REVIZOR (partly revised), the final version of his three dramatic fragments (LITIGATION, FRAGMENT, THE SERVANTS' ROOM), and HOMEGOING FROM THE THEATRE.

1846. THE DENOUEMENT OF THE REVIZOR.

1847. SELECTED PASSAGES FROM CORRESPONDENCE WITH MY FRIENDS. (Actually published on December 31st, 1846.)

After Gogol's death his literary remains were published, among which the most important are:

1. The preserved fragments of the second part of DEAD SOULS.
2. An Author's Confession.
3. Meditations on the Divine Liturgy.

CHRONOLOGICAL LIST

ENGLISH TRANSLATIONS OF GOGOL'S WORKS

The Works of Nikolay Gogol (translated by Mrs. Constance Garnett. Chatto and Windus.)

In progress:

1 & 2. *Dead Souls.*

3. *The Overcoat, and Other Stories.* (Nevsky Prospect, The Overcoat, The Carriage, A Madman's Diary, The Prisoner, The Nose, The Portrait.)

St. John's Eve, and Other Stories. Translated by J. F. Hapgood; Cromwell & Co., New York, 1886. (St. John's Eve, The Old-World Landowners, The Quarrel of the Two Ivans, The Portrait, The Cloak.)

Taras Bulba; also *St. John's Eve*, and other stories. Vizitelly and Co., New York, 1887. (The Cloak, The Quarrel of the Two Ivans, The Portrait, Viy, The Calash.)

Cossack Tales. Translated by G. Tolstoy, London, 1860. (The Night of Christmas Eve, Taras Bulba.)

Taras Bulba. Translated by J. F. Hapgood. J. W. Lowell, New York, 1888.

Taras Bulba. Translated by Baskerville. W. Scott, 1907.

Taras Bulba. W. Scott, 1916.

Taras Bulba, and Other Tales: With an Introduction by John Cournos. Everyman's Library. (Taras Bulba, The Quarrel of the Two Ivans, St. John's Eve, The Calash, The Portrait.)

The Mantle, and Other Stories. Translated by Claud Field, and with an Introduction on Gogol by Prosper Mérimée. (The Mantle, The Nose, Memoirs of a Madman, A May Night, Viy.) Werner Laurie, 1915.

A new version of *The Cloak* is to be found in *Stories from Russian Authors.* Translated by R. S. Townsend. Everyman's Library.

ENGLISH TRANSLATIONS AND EDITIONS OF *THE REVIZOR*

1. *The Inspector.* Translated by T. Hart-Davies. Thacker, Spink & Co., Calcutta, 1890.

2. *The Inspector-General*: With Introduction and Notes. By A. Sykes, 1892-93. W. Scott.

3. *Revizor.* Translated for the Yale University Dramatic Association by M. S. Mandell. With an Introduction by W. L. Phelps. Newhaven, Conn., 1910.

ENGLISH TRANSLATIONS AND EDITIONS OF *DEAD SOULS*

1. The first (mangled and distorted) English version of this work appeared during the Crimean campaign, without the author's name and under the title, *Home Life in Russia*, by a Russian nobleman. (Revised by the editor of *Revelations of Siberia*). London, 1854.

2. *Tchitchikoff's Journeys:* or, *Dead Souls.* Translated by Isabel Hapgood. Two volumes. Cromwell & Co., New York, 1886.

3. *Dead Souls.* 1887. Vizitelly & Co.

4. *Dead Souls*: With an Introduction by Stephen Graham. T. F. Unwin, London, 1915.

5. *Dead Souls.* Translated by Hogarth. With an Introduction by John Cournos. Everyman's Library.

6. The already-mentioned translation by Mrs. Constance Garnett. In two volumes. Chatto and Windus.

Of Gogol's non-fictional works, his *Meditations on the Divine Liturgy* has been translated (by Alexeieff) into English. A. R. Mowbray & Co., London, 1913.

FRENCH TRANSLATIONS

1. *Les Veillées de l'Ukraine.*" Traduit par E. Halpérine-Kaminsky. E. Flammarion, Paris, 1890. (La foire de Sorotchinetz, La nuit de mai, La nuit de la Saint Jean, La missive perdue.)

2. *Contes et Nouvelle.* Traduit par Henri Chirol. E. Flammarion, 1899. (La terrible vengeance, La place ensorcélee, Le nez, Mémoires d'un fou.)

3. *Les Veillées du hameau près de Dikanka.* Traduit par S. Lewitzka et Roger Allard. Paris, 1921.

4. *Le Manteau*. Traduit par X. Marmier in his *Au bord de la Neva*. 1856.

5. *Le Nez*. (Golschmann et Joubert. L'Ame Russe, 1896.)

6. *Mémoires d'un fou*, etc. Traduit par René Onillon. Paris. Henri Gautier. Nouvelle Bibliothèque populaire. 1893.

Taras Bulba :

1. Translated by Louis Viardot in his *Nouvelles Russes*. Paris Paulin, 1845.

The second edition (without *Taras Bulba*) was published by Hachette, in 1853, under the title : *Nouvelles choisies de Nicolas Gogol*.

2. Translated by E. Tseytline and E. Joubert. Paris. Lecène-Oudin. 1889.

3. Translated by Michel-Déline. E. Flammarion. 1891.

4. Translated by X. Paris. Librairie illustrée. 1892.

The Marriage :

1. Translated by Dénis Roches, under the title *Hyménée*. Paris. Nouvelle Revue Francaise. 1921.

2. Translated by Marc Semenoff. Paris. Plon-Nourrit. 1922

3. Translated by Gérard Gailly in his short anthology of Gogol's works, including, apart from the Introduction and Bibliography, the translations of *Nevsky Prospect*, *Confession of an Author*, *The Marriage*, and the third chapter of *Dead Souls*. The book appeared in the series *Les cent chef-d'oeuvres étrangers*. Paris. La Renaissance du livre.

The Revizor :

1. Translated by Prosper Mérimée in his volume, *Les deux héritages*. Paris. Calmann-Levy. 1853.

2. Translated by Challande. Paris. Sandoz et Fichbacher. 1868.

3. Translated by E. Gothi. Paris. Ollendorf. 1893.

4. Translated by Ernest Combes. Paris. Larousse. 1918.

5. Translated by Marc Semenoff. Paris. Plon-Nourrit. 1922.

GOGOL

Dead Souls:

1. Translated by Eugène Moreau. Paris. Harvard. 1858.
2. Translated by Ernest Charrière. Paris. Hachette. 1859
3. Various extracts from *Dead Souls* were translated also by Prosper Mérimée (in 1851), Louis Léger, Gérard Gailly, etc.

SOME GERMAN TRANSLATIONS

One of the first stories of Gogol translated into German was his *Quarrel of the Two Ivans*, which appeared in Lippert's *Nordisches Novellenbuch*. 1846.

His *Nevsky Prospect* appeared in 1868, in *Pentameron*.

Cheap editions of Gogol's works in German can be obtained in Reclam's Universal Bibliothek. They include the following volumes:

1. *Phantasien und Geschichten*. 4 vols. Translated by W. Lange.
2. *Taras Bulba*. Translated by W. Lange.
3. *Die toten Seelen*. Translated by Loebenstein.

SOME ITALIAN TRANSLATIONS

1. *Taras Bulba*. Milano. 1877. (In Farina's *Scelta di buoni romanzi stranieri*.)
2. *Le Anime Morte*. Rome. 1882.
3. *Roma*. Novelle Ucraine. Lettere. Florence. 1883.

Apart from the above-mentioned versions, Gogol's works have been translated into practically all other European languages. He is a special favourite with the Slavs, particularly Czechs. His *Revizor* can be obtained also in Esperanto, translated by Dr. Zamenhof himself.

BIBLIOGRAPHY

SOME RUSSIAN EDITIONS OF GOGOL'S WORKS

The first edition of Gogol's works appeared in four volumes in 1842 (Petersburg). Since then numerous editions have been published, the most important of which are:

WORKS AND LETTERS. Published by Kulish in six volumes. 1857.

GOGOL'S WORKS. Edited by Tikhonravov and partly by Shenrok. (Petersburg. 1889–96–7.)

GOGOL'S WORKS. Edited by V. V. Kallash in ten volumes. (Petrograd. 1915.) Brockhaus-Efron.

COMPLETE WORKS OF GOGOL. In one volume. Edited by Tikhonravov and Shenrok. 1919.

Gogol's letters were collected and edited by Shenrok in four volumes. (Petersburg.) 1902.

SOME OF THE RUSSIAN WORKS ON GOGOL

Aksakov, S. — *History of my Acquaintance with Gogol, including our Correspondence.* 1832–52. Moscow, 1890 and 1891.

Annenkov, P. — *Literary Reminiscences* (*Gogol in Rome*). Petersburg. 1909.

Alexandrovsky, G. — Gogol's *Revizor.* Kiev. 1898.

Annensky, I. — On the forms of the fantastic in Gogol. (*The Russian School.* 1890.)
The Problem of Gogol's Humour (In his *Book of Reflections.* 1906.)
The Esthetics of *The Dead Souls*.(In *Apollon.*) 1911.

GOGOL

Bagaley, D.	Evolution of Gogol's Artistic Creation. (In *Vyestnik Evropy.*) 1909.
Bazhenov, N.	*Gogol's Illness and Death.* Moscow. 1903.
Biely, A.	Gogol (In his *Green Meadow*). 1910.
Bielinsky, V.	Articles on Gogol. (Various editions of Bielinsky's works.)
Brussov, V.	*Ispepelyonny* (The Man who Burnt Himself out). Moscow. 1909.
Chernishevsky, N.	Sketches of Gogol's Time. (Chernishevsky's Works) 1906.
Czizh, V.	Gogol's Disease. (In *Problems of Philosophy and Psychology.*) 1903.
Eichenbaum, B.	How *The Cloak* was written. (In *Poetica.*) 1919. Petrograd.
Gershenzon, M.	Gogol's Bequest. (In *Russkaya Mysl.*) 1909.
Grigoryev, A.	Gogol and his *Correspondence with Friends.* 1915.
Hippius, V.	*Gogol.* 1924.
Ivanov, I.	*Gogol, the Man and the Writer.* Kiev. 1909.
Kallash, V. V.	*Gogol.* As recorded by his contemporaries and his correspondence. 1909.
Kirpichnikov, A.	*Doubts and Contradictions in Gogol's Biography.* Petersburg. 1902.
Kolomiytsev, V.	Gogol in Music. (In the *Messenger of Theatre and Art.*) Petersburg. 1921.
Korolenko, V.	A Writer's Tragedy. (In *Russkoe Bogatsvo.*) 1909.
Kotlyarevsky, N. A.	*Gogol.* Petrograd. 1915.
Lvov, V.	*Gogol in the Reminiscences of his Contemporaries.* Moscow. 1909.
Lukyanovsky, P. B.	*Pushkin and Gogol.* Moscow. 1915.
M. Nicholas. (P. A. Kulish.)	*An Attempt at Gogol's Biography, including Forty of His Letters.* 1854.
Mandelshtam, I.	*The Character of Gogol's Style.* Helsingfors. 1902.
Markovsky.	*History of the Origin and Creation of* The Dead Souls. Kiev. 1902.

BIBLIOGRAPHY

Merezhkovsky, D. *Gogol and the Devil.* 1906.

Nevirova, E. *Themes from Ukrainian Demonology in Gogol's* Evenings *and* Mirgorod. (In Little Russian.) 1909.

Ovsyaniko-Kulikovsky. *Gogol.* (Latest edition published by the State Publishing Company.) 1923.

Pereverzev, V. *Gogol's Creation.* 1914.

Pokrovsky, V. I. *Gogol.* 1908.

Priluko-Prilutsky. *Gogol:* A Compilation in the series *Masters of the Russian Language. No.* 8.

Rozanov, V. Two articles on Gogol in his Study of Dostoevsky's *Grand Inquisitor.* Petersburg 1894.

Gogol and his Significance for the Theatre. (In his book *Among Artists*). Petersburg. 1902.

Rozov, V. *Traditional Types of the Little Russian Theatre of the Seventeenth and Eighteenth Centuries, and Gogol's First Stories.* Kiev. 1912.

Scheglov, I. *A Champion of the Word.* (New materials about Gogol.) Petersburg. 1909.

Schegolev, P. *Gogol's Childhood.* Petersburg. 1913.

Shenrok, V. J. *Material for a Biography of Gogol.* (Four vols.) 1902–8.

Slonimsky, A. *The Technique of Gogol's Humour.* Petrograd. 1923.

Smirnov, V. *On the Literary History of* The Revizor. (Reports of the Academy of Sciences.) 1901.

Smirnovsky. *Gogol: His Life and his Literary Activity.* Petersburg. 1896.

Sollogub (Count). *Reminiscences of Gogol, Pushkin, Lermontov.* 1866.

Tarasenkov, A. *Gogol's Last Days.* Petersburg. 1857.

Tynyanov, J. *Dostoevsky and Gogol.* Petrograd. 1921.

Yermakov, Prof. *Studies in the Psychology of Gogol's Creation.* 1923.

Dead Souls: A Psycho-analytical treatment of the novel (its publication announced).

GOGOL

Varneke. *History of the Russian Theatre.* (2 vols.) Kazan. 1908–10.

Vengerov, P. *Gogol as Writer and as Citizen.* 1907.

Vesselovsky, A. *Studies and Characteristics.* Moscow. 1907.

Veinberg, L. *Gogol.* (A collection of articles from Kireyevsky to Eichenwald.) Petersburg. 1913.

Vinogradov, V. The Subject and the Composition of the Story *The Nose.* (In *Nachala.*) 1921.

Vladimirov, P. V. *An Essay on Gogol's Evolution.* Kiev. 1891. *On the History of Russian Comedy.* Petersburg. 1899.

Zielinsky, V. A. *Russian Critical Literature on Gogol's Works.* (3 vols.)

Zolotaryov, S. *Gogol's Russia.* 1909.

Various collections of articles and essays on Gogol were published by the Russian Academy and universities, etc.

More or less interesting articles on Gogol and his works can be found in books dealing with modern Russian literature, particularly in the work of Pypin, Speransky, Ivanov-Razumnik, etc. etc.

ARTICLES ON GOGOL IN ENGLISH

The best-known essays on Gogol in English are those by Maurice Baring in his two books : *Landmarks in Russian Literature* (Methuen, 1910), and *A History of Russian Literature* (Home University Library).

There are appreciations of Gogol in books dealing with Russian literature by A. Bruckner, Waliszewsky, Prince Kropotkin, and recently in a concise little volume on Modern Russian Literature by Prince D. S. Mirsky (*Oxford World Manuals.*) A useful contribution is the English translation of M. de Vogüé's book, *The Russian Novel.* Translated by Col. H. A. Sawyer. Chapman & Hall. 1913.

BIBLIOGRAPHY

SOME FRENCH WORKS ON GOGOL.

Ernest Charrière's	Preface to his translation of *Dead Souls.* Paris. 1859.
Ernest Dupuy.	*Les grands maîtres de la littérature russe au XIXe siècle.* Paris. Lecène et Oudin. 1885.
Louis Leger.	*Nicolas Gogol.* Paris. Bloud. 1914.
Osip Lourié.	*La psychologie des romanciers russes du XIXe siècle.* Paris. Alkan. 1905.
Prosper Mérimée.	*La littérature en Russie.* (Revue des Deux Mondes, 15 novembre 1851, and also as an appendix to his *Carmen.* 1852.)
Patouillet.	*Le Théatre de moeurs russes des origines à Ostrovsky.* Paris. H. Champion. 1912. *Ostrovsky et son théatre de moeurs russes.* Paris. Plon-Nourrit. 1912.
Sainte-Beuve.	*Nicolas Gogol.* Premiers Lundis, t. 3. The article is dated December 1st, 1845, and deals with Louis Viardot's *Nouvelles russes.* Paris. Calmann-Levy. 1891.
O. N. Smirnova.	*Etudes et Souvenirs* in *La Nouvelle Revue.* Paris. 1885.
Raina Tyrneva.	*Nicolas Gogol, écrivain et moraliste.* A thesis. Aix. Makaire. 1901.
Melchior de Vogüé.	*La roman russe.* Paris. Plon-Nourrit. 1886.
Melchior de Vogüé et Louis Léger.	*Inauguration du monument élevé à la mémoire de Nicolas Gogol à Moscou le neuf mai 1909.* Paris. Firmin Didot. 1909.
Theodor de Wyzewa.	*Ecrivains étrangers.* 2me serie. Paris. 1897.

There are numerous studies on Gogol in German of which may be mentioned :

Delle Grazie.	The ninth volume of his *Sämmtliche Werke.* Leipzig. 1903–4.
Otto Kaus.	*Der Fall Gogol.* Munich. 1912.

GOGOL

A. Pypin. *Die Bedeutung Gogols fur die heutige internationale Stellung der russischen Literatur.* (Archiv fur Slav. Philologie. 1903. 2, XV.)

Thiess, F. *Gogol und seine Bühnenwerke.* 1922.

E. Zabel. *Russische Literaturbilder.* Berlin. 1899.

A good essay on Gogol is to be found also in the Dutch book by N. van Wyk, *Hoofdmomenten der Russiese letterkunde.* 1919.

INDEX

INDEX

INDEX